Care of the Horse

Care of the Horse

John Bullock

Country Life

By the same author:
The Horse and Pony Quiz Book

With Robert Owen:
The Horse and Pony Gift Book
Buying and Keeping a Horse or Pony
Caring for a Horse or Pony
Riding and Schooling
About Jumping
The Young Rider

The author is indebted to Francesca Bullock, Jacky Thomas, and Anne-Marie and Richard Hancock for helping to illustrate the book.

Published by Country Life Books
Holman House 95 Sheen Road
Richmond upon Thames Surrey TW9 1YJ
and distributed for them by
The Hamlyn Publishing Group Limited
London · New York · Sydney · Toronto
Astronaut House Feltham Middlesex England

First printed in 1980

A Grisewood and Dempsey Book
produced for the publisher

© **Grisewood and Dempsey Ltd 1980**
Grosvenor House, 141/143 Drury Lane
London WC2

ISBN 0 600 32216 5

Set in 10 point Century Schoolbook by Computer Photoset Ltd, Birmingham, England
Printed and bound by South China Printing Co, Hong Kong

Acknowledgements
The photographs in this book are used by courtesy of the following people and organizations:
Equestrian (Photographic) Services Ltd: Cover,2,4,6,11,13 top,17,19,20,22,24,25,26, 27,29,31,32,34,35,43,44,45,47,49,50,52, 53,55,56-59,62-65,67,69,70-71,72,73,75, 77,78,80-81,83,85,91,94,95,98,102,105, 106,109, back cover.
Equestrian (Press and General) Services Ltd: 8,13 bottom, 40,41,74,79,96
Alfred Spencer: 15,48
Sally-Ann Thompson: 21,37,61,89,101,107, 108
Zefa: 92

Contents

Introduction

Horses, like people, vary in size, temperament, strength, scope and ability. What is right for one animal may not be suitable for another. By varying training, exercise, diet and even on occasions companions and surroundings, a successful owner or trainer learns how to get the best response, according to the facilities available and the work each horse is expected to do.

In keeping any horse, there are, however, some rules which should be followed to ensure his welfare, irrespective of whether he is to be used for polo, horse trials, show jumping, hunting, showing or driving, or just as a pleasant hack. This book deals with these essentials; but at the same time it provides advice as to how to assess the particular needs of each individual animal, and how to introduce variety into the care of the horse in order not only to achieve the best results, but also to get the most enjoyment from horse ownership.

All successful trainers have their own theories and methods, which they have developed through years of experience in their own particular activity or sport. Their views may differ, but they use the individual knowledge they have gained to save time and money or to help them towards producing horses at a higher peak of fitness and ability than those of other competitors. That is part of the fun of training. The more time spent with horses, the greater the realization of how much more there is to learn.

This book is intended to provide a sound basis on which to build that experience.

The decision whether to keep a horse stabled or out at grass depends on a number of factors. A Thoroughbred point-to-pointer such as this needs to be stabled, and his owner must be able to afford the time and money to look after him properly.

7

1: Stabled or at grass: the choice

Circumstances play an important part in all horse ownership. People living in a town are hardly likely to have acres of pasture land available, and keeping a horse at livery some way from their home may be the only sensible answer. Even people who live in the country, and who have land and stabling available, may have problems of time or money that influence their decision as to the type of animal to buy and the way in which he will have to be kept.

The rider's own ambition and ability must also be a consideration. If you are considering buying a horse you must ask yourself certain fundamental questions: for example, what do I want to do with him? Do I really want to compete, and if so at what standard? If I am hoping to hunt, and can do so only occasionally, am I prepared to accept the fact that I will have to turn for home when my horse has had enough, even if hounds are still running?

Of course, if you are buying a pony the decision on how to keep him may be easier to make, because most ponies do better at grass, leading an outdoor life, so long as they have adequate, well-fenced grazing that is not too lush in summer. The only other essential requirements are a constant supply of clean water, and a suitable field shelter to provide protection from the sun and flies in summer, and the wind and driving rain in winter.

An animal at grass will still need daily attention, of course. But his requirements will be modest compared with those of a stabled horse, which will need daily

A horse that is expected to compete in a demanding three day event has to be extremely fit and must obviously be stabled. This type of horse is trained to a high standard of obedience, not only for the dressage phase, but also for the steeplechasing, cross-country and show jumping phases. Horses do not like jumping into water, particularly when they cannot see the bottom and do not know what they are jumping into. But a horse can be trained to overcome his reluctance and have faith in his rider and his rider's instructions.

exercise and grooming, at least three feeds a day, clean bedding, a change of rugs and probably more frequent visits from the blacksmith.

The best solution for many owners, with only limited time available, may be to stable a horse or pony for part of the time, and turn him out when he is not needed. Some people call this the 'half-and-half' or 'combined' system, and provided that they do not own a blood horse and are not going to be too ambitious and expect too much, there is a great deal to recommend it.

The secret of successful ownership is for both horse and rider to be contented. A contented horse is more likely to keep in good condition and to do his best without getting into mischief; and a contented rider will not try to tax an animal too much–expecting him to perform tasks when he is not fit enough, or has not the scope or training to be able to tackle his work properly.

The combined system

The best method of keeping a horse or pony is to stable by day in the summer and by night in winter, and let him spend the rest of the time turned out in a field. In this way, the animal only really requires attention early in the morning and in the evening.

It is not even necessary to have a fully equipped stable, provided that a field shelter can be adapted so that the horse can be shut up when required. It must be constructed in such a way that he can see out easily and get plenty of fresh air.

As a rule, ponies kept at grass still need a stable or shelter where they can be shut in if necessary when they are getting too fat, or on the night before they are due to go hunting or to a gymkhana. Mobile stables are now available which can be towed behind a horsebox or car, and used in a field without the need for planning permission.

A horse that is kept in at night during the winter will be dry in the morning, ready to be groomed and ridden as soon as it becomes light. Similarly, after being kept in during the day in summer, he will be all ready to be ridden in the cool of the evening, when his rider returns from work.

This system allows a horse to be partially clipped in winter to allow faster work, provided that he has a waterproof New Zealand rug when he is turned out, and a jute rug for the stable. He can also be kept very much fitter because it is possible to restrict the amount of lush grass he has in summer: he will not get fat and risk such illnesses as laminitis. In winter he can be fed hay, as well as concentrates in the form of oats, nuts and bran that give him added energy.

It will, of course, be necessary to keep the stable or field shelter clean, to keep bedding fresh and to ensure water is always available. But there will be less need for regular exercise and grooming.

The stable-kept horse

If time and money are no problem, a very satisfactory way of keeping a horse is to have him stabled day and night, so that he is ready to be ridden at virtually any time. He can be kept fully fit and able to do hard, fast work as and when required.

Apart from a suitable stable, he will require day and night rugs (and a blanket in the winter), water buckets, a feed bowl and mucking-out equipment, according to whether he is being kept on straw, peat or shavings. There must also be a good supply of hay and bedding, and a dry and vermin-proof store where his concentrates and other foodstuff can be kept.

Because of the variety of saddlery and other equipment which will be needed, it would be advisable to have a tack room that can be locked and made as thief proof as possible. Good saddlery is expensive and there is a lucrative business in stolen tack, so break-ins are becoming common.

Top: If a horse is not used to dogs accompanying him, he will feel nervous and may behave badly. The rider must make sure that the horse overcomes any such fear before going out onto the road.

Right: Horses that are turned out to grass take the exercise they need. Frequent exercising is not so necessary.

Electricity will have to be laid on to the stables, fodder store and tack room to allow the horse to be worked on during the winter months when there are only a few hours of daylight. Power will also be needed, of course, for clipping.

A stabled horse needs regular grooming and exercise. The amount of exercise depends upon the work he is being asked to do. A horse or pony hunting two or three days a week will obviously need less daily exercise than an animal that is only used for hacking, or is only being taken to occasional competitions. But, on average, a stabled horse needs about one and a half to two hours' gentle exercise a day with a 'pipe opener' about twice a week.

Exercise is essential for health because it improves circulation, stimulates digestion and helps the horse's general well-being. It improves the flow of blood to the feet and limbs–an important consideration in trying to avoid various disorders. And apart from keeping the animal fit, it prevents boredom, so long as the ride is varied every day.

A bored horse very quickly becomes a nuisance, and boredom can lead to bad vices, such as crib biting, wind sucking and weaving.

When regularly stabled, a horse needs a minimum of two hard feeds a day, in addition to hay. Shoeing charges tend to be high because of the amount of road work that is done.

An outlet for the stabled horse

Even when a horse is stabled, it is advisable to have a field handy where he can be turned out for 10 or 20 minutes each day, usually after he has been ridden, so that he can have a good roll and let off steam. A few mouthfuls of grass will do him good, and he will look forward to his few minutes of relaxation without anyone on his back to make him behave.

If he proves difficult to catch he should be left wearing a headcollar with a short piece of rope attached, so that there is something to hold on to when you go up to him with a bowl of nuts or oats. But horses that are allowed a few minutes' freedom each day are not usually difficult to catch after the first two or three days, except when the grass is particularly sweet in the spring. The problem usually occurs only when horses are allowed their freedom very occasionally.

If there is not a field available, let him have a nibble of grass along the verge of a road, provided that the road is quiet and he is not bad with traffic. Make sure, however, that you always put yourself between the horse and the road, and that he has a good headcollar and either a strong rope or a chain. A rope is preferable because a chain can cut your hand if a horse starts to play about; but never wrap a rope around your hand. Fortunately, a horse kept in the stable will usually be too interested in filling his stomach with grass to want to misbehave.

The half-and-half system is certainly the answer for people who have limited time and capital, but who would still like to keep their own horse. However, for those who have ambitions to compete seriously or to hunt two or three days a week, the only answer is a stable and an alarm clock.

Right: Large cross-country fences and combinations must be jumped accurately with complete understanding between horse and rider.

Competition horses need training periods in addition to their regular exercise. A horse can be schooled over upright poles to teach him to jump accurately, and to take off when his rider tells him. This is a difficult type of schooling jump, because there is no ground line to help the horse judge his stride.

2: The horse at grass

Grassland is affected by four factors: climate, height above sea level, soil and grass management. The only factor that is in the hands of an owner is management, but it is an aspect that many are inclined to ignore. A horse cannot just be turned loose in a paddock and be left to fend for himself, even though grazing is his natural way of life. The grass that he needs only grows well when there is sufficient moisture, warmth and sunlight, and its nutritive value varies considerably from season to season.

In the wild, horses can forage and look for other food in winter when grass is not available. But it is noticeable that the ponies that run wild in various places and have to fend for themselves rarely thrive, and do not always even survive the winter.

A domesticated horse or pony in an enclosed field has little opportunity of finding other food when the grass is short or the goodness has gone from it. From autumn to late spring he will need extra food in the form of hay, as well as regular feeds of concentrates such as oats or perhaps nuts mixed with bran.

In the spring and early summer, the reverse is usually the case. The grass is highly nutritious, particularly in early summer, and animals left to feed at will tend to eat too much lush grass. As a result, they become over-fat and are more likely to suffer from diseases caused by obesity. The most common of these is laminitis or 'fever of the feet'. Small, fat ponies are particularly susceptible to this danger; but any type or size of horse can become affected, and horses should be turned out for only limited periods until the grass becomes less nutritious.

How horses feed

Horses living out at grass tend to settle into a fixed routine. Usually, they graze between 16 and 18 hours a day, depending on the quality of the grass and the time of year. On an average day, a horse can probably get through as much as 25 kgs (50 lb) or more of grass. A medium-sized pony will eat slightly less.

Horses will doze standing up, particularly if there is not room to lie down or if the ground is too wet and muddy. But they usually like to lie down when they have somewhere comfortable to stretch out. This is particularly obvious in the summer, when they will lie fully stretched out in the sun soaking up the warmth.

During the summer, horses out at grass usually also lie down for a few hours during the night or early in the morning, when few people are about to see them. In the winter they walk about at night to keep warm, and only lie down during the warmest part of the day, usually about midday. Consequently, many people think that horses lie down to sleep more in winter than in summer; but this is not so.

The most concentrated period of eating takes place just after dawn and before dusk, when the dew is on the grass. Horses do not graze much when it is really dark. It is because of this that ponies seem to get out of their fields more often at night than

Horses need daily attention even when turned out at grass. Apart from shelter and an adequate supply of clean water, they should have additional feed in the form of hay and concentrates during the autumn and winter months when the nutritional value of the grass is low. But if a horse's field has too much lush grass during the spring and summer months, his grazing time should be restricted.

in daytime: they are wandering about trying to keep warm and have nothing much to do.

During the day and after he has had his early morning graze and rest, a horse will probably spend quite a lot of time moving about his field at random. During his wandering, he will pick at the grass rather than eat continuously. This tendency to 'pick'–at a time when many people are about to see them–tends to give horses a reputation for being bad grazers. As a rule, horses are inclined to eat the most tasty grasses, leaving the ones they do not like. These rejected patches grow tall. This is particularly true of the areas of grass around horse droppings.

The quality of grazing

Most horses and ponies do best on moderate land. Very rich pastures are not good. The best types of pasture for horses will contain such grasses as Meadow Fescue, which when fully established is very palatable; perennial Rye grass, which has valuable qualities; White Clover, which helps other grasses by nitrogen fixation and is also tasty and does well in dry areas; Red Clover, which is very palatable and able to cope well in drought conditions; and Timothy grass, which grows well once it is properly established and which comes up in early spring.

Most fields also contain a great many other grasses that are more common but have little or no nutritional value. These include Yorkshire Fog, Tall Fescue, Wild Cocksfoot and rough-stalked meadow grasses that smother the more productive grasses during their short growing period.

Then there are the weeds that everyone would like to get rid of: thistles, stinging nettles, docks and so on. The only way to deal with them is by regular cutting before they seed or by spraying with weedkiller when the fields are being rested.

Dangerous plants

Poisonous trees and plants are a more serious problem than weeds, and a careful watch for them must be kept on all fields being grazed by horses. This is particularly important if a field is to be used for hay, because some plants (Ragwort, for instance) are a greater menace dead than alive.

Fortunately, Ragwort, which usually grows in sunny parts of the field rather than in the hedgerows, can be pulled up quite easily, roots and all, and burnt or put into the safety of a dustbin. Ragwort damages the liver of a horse or pony that eats it, but the poisoning takes effect slowly. For this reason, it is unwise to buy an animal that has been grazing in a field full of Ragwort, although a horse will not usually eat the plant if there is plenty of good grass available.

Plants that prefer damp ditches and hedgerows, such as Deadly Nightshade and members of the hemlock family (including Cowbane and Water Dropwort) are just as poisonous but are more difficult to deal with. They must be removed quickly, preferably by someone wearing gloves. They are at their most dangerous when they begin to wilt; that is when animals seem to be most tempted by them. Privet, too, is poisonous and a horse should not be allowed near hedge trimmings. Grass cuttings can also cause serious problems to a horse's digestion and must never be fed under any circumstances.

Yew is very poisonous, but horses seem more inclined to feed on a branch that has been blown down in a storm than from a tree growing in a hedge. The best advice that can be given to anyone with yew trees where horses are to graze is to get rid of them. It is better to be safe than sorry, and there are plenty of other beautiful trees that will not do any harm.

Even oaks can cause problems if they shed large quantities of acorns. These can be eaten by a hungry horse or pony with fatal results. If there is an oak tree in the field where your horse grazes, watch out

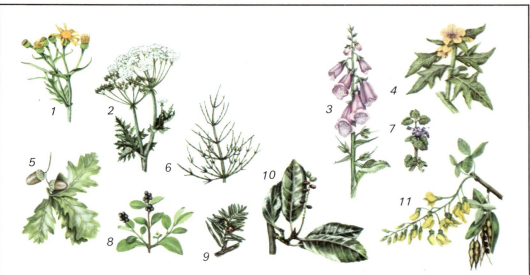

Horse owners must learn to recognize common trees, plants and weeds that are poisonous to horses and in some cases can even prove fatal. Seeds carry easily with the wind, and it is important to check fields regularly to ensure that they are trouble free. If there is an oak tree in the field or hedgerow, acorn time requires special vigilance, particularly when the wind is strong. Many horses and ponies enjoy acorns but are poisoned by them. Dangerous plants to look for include:

1 Ragwort   2 Hemlock
3 Foxglove   4 Henbane   5 Oak (acorns)
6 Horsetail   7 Ground ivy   8 Privet
9 Yew   10 Laurel   11 Laburnum

Dangerous plants should never be cut down with a sickle, but must be pulled up by the roots and either burnt or put into a dustbin out of the way. Some plants, such as ragwort, are far more dangerous dead than when they are growing. Some other weeds, such as thistles, stinging nettles and docks, must be dealt with quickly to prevent them spreading. They can either be sprayed with weedkiller, or cut down regularly before they have a chance to seed.

for strong winds and gales. If acorns start to drop in large numbers, collect them up before the horse has time to get to them.

Maintaining the pasture

Pastures can become horse-sick if they are not properly looked after. A field that has had horses on it for a long time and has been poorly maintained becomes very patchy, with tufts of long grass that horses would sooner go hungry than eat. These fields can also become a dangerous source of worms' eggs.

Horses tend to deposit their droppings in certain areas; their aversion to these areas when grazing is certainly a help in preventing the spread of the worm parasites that inhabit an animal's gut and live on the food that passes through. A horse with worms does not get proper benefit from the food it eats, so that it quickly becomes poor and listless.

All horses and ponies, whether living out or in a stable, must be wormed at least three times a year. Equine worms are very prolific, and produce large quantities of microscopic eggs that pass out with the droppings and can quickly contaminate a field. Young horses are particularly susceptible.

The best solution is to graze cattle for a time in the field with the horses. Cattle graze much more evenly; and, as they do not have any front top teeth, they tear the grass out in bunches instead of biting it off neatly like a horse. Because they have such excellent frontal teeth or incisors, horses are able to bite off blades of grass low down to the ground, so that areas of grass can become very bare, and take time to recover.

Fortunately, cattle with their different methods of grazing will quite happily eat infected grass. The eggs die as soon as they are eaten, and the cattle will not become affected. Nor will sheep. There is also little risk of horses being affected by cattle or sheep worms.

Before putting cattle in a field, however, it is important to make sure that all the fencing is secure. If one animal forces his way through a gap the others will follow.

If the field is not too large, it is sometimes worthwhile spending an hour or so once a week picking up the horse droppings in a wheelbarrow, and carting them off to the manure heap. Regular chain harrowing will help to disperse the dung, and at the same time expose the parasites to the cold and light. The field should also be rolled. If cattle are not available, the areas of long grass should be 'topped' either by hand or by mower, depending on the size of the field.

Resting grassland regularly is important. Each horse or pony requires about 0.8 hectare (2 acres) if he is going to live out all the year round. And it is as well to divide a field into two and let each half be grazed alternately, rather than have the whole area used at one time. It is also easier to keep the droppings under control if one half of the field is given an opportunity to recover naturally while the other is being grazed.

Cattle are very useful in keeping fields sweet for horses. They graze quite differently, and can eat infected grass without any harmful effects.

If there is a shortage of good grazing, it is important to keep a field as free as possible of horse droppings, because they will quickly sour the grass. A weekly visit with a wheelbarrow can help in keeping a field in good condition. The droppings should be collected and taken off to the muck heap before they have time to cause trouble.

The area of grassland required will depend on the type of soil. Clay for example, gets very wet and boggy during the winter, and horses are more likely to get mud fever. Their sharp hooves quickly cut up the ground, causing large muddy patches round water troughs, gateways and shelter entrances.

In the summer clay becomes very hard, and in very dry periods large cracks will appear. Under such circumstances 0.8 hectare (2 acres) per horse becomes an absolute minimum requirement, however much hay and concentrates are fed.

One answer to the problem would be to try to rent another field somewhere nearby which can be grazed in the very wet weather. Preferably, it should be a field with a different kind of soil.

Fencing and hedges

Whatever type of paddock or pasture is being used, it will need to be properly fenced, not only for the safety of the horse but also to prevent other people's property

19

being damaged. A horse owner who lets his animals stray through bad management will become very unpopular with his neighbours, and will risk legal penalties. He will also be doing a disservice to other horse owners in general by giving them a bad name.

Good sound hedges, free of poisonous trees and plants, or solid post and rail fencing about 1.5 metres (4 ft) in height, with easily opened wood or metal gates are, of course, ideal. Hedges, however, take time to grow unless they are already well established and post and rail fencing is expensive. As an alternative, wooden or concrete posts with heavy-gauge smooth wire pulled tight are very effective. But wire that is not drawn tight can be very dangerous, because horses can so easily get entangled in it. A fence must be properly erected, with the posts set firmly in the ground, and the lowest strand of wire should be a minimum of 0.5 metres (18 in) high so that it is easily visible and will not get caught in a horse's shoe.

Barbed wire is not to be recommended. Neither is electric fencing, which becomes useless if the battery gets flat or if the wire is broken.

I do not like teaching horses to be frightened of wire, particularly if they are to go hunting. A very great deal of wire is being used in fencing today; and on the occasions when it is necessary to put a coat over some wire and jump it, the rider does not want a horse that will shy away in fear.

Barbed wire can cause serious injury to horses and if there is any around a field used for grazing it should be removed and replaced with post and rail fencing. Loose strands are particularly dangerous. Horses are inclined to put their heads through strands of wire in a fence to reach fresh areas of grass or juicy shoots; even if the wire is taut their manes will become entangled in it.

Water and shelter

A good supply of clean water is also essential in a field being grazed. Domestic baths do not make good water troughs, because horses can damage themselves on the lips if they get their feet underneath. But, of course, the sides of the bath can be boarded-in to prevent this.

Field shelters need not be palatial affairs, but they do need to have good wide openings and plenty of headroom, and to be solid enough to stand up to a horse rubbing against them. It is also important to ensure that there are not any sharp protrusions. Horses at grass enjoy having a good rub from time to time, and a sharp nail or piece of metal can do a lot of damage.

I once had a little Thoroughbred mare tear an eyelid in two by rubbing her head against a piece of wood with a small piece of metal embedded in it, which I had not noticed. Fortunately, some brilliant stitching by a skilful veterinary surgeon

saved her beauty and her sight; but it was a painful lesson.

Corrugated iron roofs for field shelters are not to be recommended because they get so hot in summer. A good felt-covered wooden roof is much better; or if that is not possible, a roof made of asbestos sheeting.

Checking the ground

Finally, before putting a horse or pony into a field go carefully over the ground to ensure that there are no bottles or pieces of old machinery that might cause injury. Horses are basically quite sensible animals, and they will usually cope with rabbit holes, mole hills and rough ground, provided that they are not galloped over it. They can, however, quite easily damage themselves by treading on hidden glass or bits of iron and wire netting. It is far better to check first, and take the trouble to remove any dangerous object, than to find a horse on three legs and have to face heavy vet's bills.

Horses need somewhere to shelter from bad weather in winter and flies in summer. A good field shelter is the best solution. The roof should have plenty of height, and the opening at the front needs to be wide enough for animals to get in and out easily without knocking themselves. This is particularly important if there are several horses in the same field. They may become fractious and chase each other in and out of a shelter. Corrugated iron roofs are not satisfactory, not only because they are inclined to rust but also because they make the shelter too hot for comfortable use in sunny weather.

3: Stabling and stable equipment

Trying to keep a horse or pony without the necessary facilities for looking after him properly can only lead to worry and disappointment, and to unnecessary veterinary bills. What facilities are needed will, of course, depend on the type of animal you have decided to keep and the job you want him to do. If you are purchasing a new horse, make up your mind whether you intend to keep him at grass all the year round or whether he will be stabled, either for the whole time or during the winter.

As a general rule, Thoroughbreds and Arabs do not winter out satisfactorily. They need careful looking after to keep them in good condition. Cobs and horses with a cross of cart-horse blood can do quite well at grass throughout the year, provided they receive the necessary daily attention and have the right facilities. The same is true of ponies of the mountain or moorland type.

Having purchased an animal that suits your pocket and ambitions, it is vitally important to feed and manage him correctly. If you do not, his condition and manners will deteriorate rapidly.

Horses are hardy creatures and can live and thrive under conditions that are far from natural to them. I have seen them stabled quite happily in towns, far from

any grassland. But there are, nevertheless, limits to their adaptability, and these limits must be realized or things will go badly wrong. When this happens, the expense to the owner and the hardship to the horse could almost always have been avoided if the owner had had a knowledge of stable management and an understanding of how horses should be kept.

The most suitable types of stabling
Stables need not necessarily be smart and expensive provided that they are of the right size and are draughtproof, light, airy and well drained. They must also be

Because of high building costs, wooden stables have become very popular. They must, however be well constructed, and have a wide enough canopy at the front to provide shelter against the rain and sun. These horses look very contented and can enjoy one another's company.

free of low beams or projections on which the horse can injure himself. And they must have adequate and safe stable fittings, and be strong enough to withstand the full weight of a horse's body when he leans against the side or gets down to roll. This may seem elementary, but I have seen horses push out the front of a wooden loose box that has been badly constructed, and break up a wall that has not had the right support.

Stalls are less popular nowadays than they were in the past, and most private owners prefer loose boxes, where their horses have more freedom of movement. If, however, you have to use a building that was not designed as stabling, it may be more satisfactory to turn it into stalls rather than into a loose box.

In a stall, the horse is tied up with his head to the wall, and secured with a headcollar by means of a rope fastened to the back 'D' of the noseband. The other end is passed through a ring, usually about

chest high, and secured by a knot to a wooden log. This method allows the rope limited freedom of movement through the ring, but prevents it getting tangled up with the horse's feet.

Stalls are usually about 2 metres (6 ft) wide and 3.5 metres (12 ft) long with a 2 metre (6 ft) passage behind. They must give the horse plenty of headroom, and they usually have a slightly sloped floor to help the drainage.

Loose boxes also need a minimum of 3 metres (10 ft) of headroom, with a floor area about 3.5 metres by 3.5 metres (12 ft by 12 ft). This allows a horse plenty of room to lie down, but is economical so far as bedding is concerned and easy to keep clean. A lower roof may cause the horse to bang his head, and the volume of air will be reduced, making the stable hot and stuffy. I have found, however, that horses sometimes get into more trouble in larger boxes, probably because they are less careful as to how and where they lie down. They are also more inclined to roll and get themselves stuck against the wall, so that they cannot get up without assistance. This is known as being *cast*.

It is as well to know how to deal with an animal that is cast without doing damage to yourself or the horse. Someone will be required to sit gently on the horse's head to keep him quiet while you talk soothingly to him: he will probably have got himself into a state of panic. You should then loop two pieces of strong rope round the fetlocks of the legs nearest to the wall. With a gentle steady pull on the ropes, it should be possible to pull the horse over until he can get to his feet. Care must be taken however to ensure you do not cause him any injury by jerking on the ropes too quickly.

Then run the horse up and see that he moves easily and evenly, after first making sure he has no particular tender areas on his back. If in any doubt, have him checked over by the veterinary surgeon. It could save money and problems later.

A smart brick-built yard with well constructed and well ventilated stables which, however, lack proper protection against driving rain.

Choosing a stable

Brick-built stables and those built of solid concrete blocks are, of course, by far the best. They look nicer, last longer and are usually completely draughtproof and windproof. Rats and mice cannot gnaw through the walls, and, because they have better insulation, they are usually warmer in winter and cooler in summer.

The cost of constructing stables made of bricks or concrete blocks may be too great for most owners. Fortunately, however, some very good stabling of the sectional wooden type is available. It varies considerably in quality and price.

The sections need only be bolted together on a suitable concrete base; as a result, their erection is a relatively quick and simple job. This type of stabling can also be provided with separate tack rooms, fodder stores and hay barns, and most of them are designed to allow for extensions.

Whatever type of stable you use, make sure that there is a large enough overhang on the roof to give protection from the rain when the horse has his head out over the stable door. The overhang also stops the inside of the box from getting wet.

Most prefabricated stables have been treated against rot. But they need to be lined with strong boards to above kicking height to prevent the walls being damaged.

The roofs are usually made of wood covered with felt, or of ridged asbestos sheeting. Corrugated iron roofs are not to be recommended, not only because they rust, but also because they get hot in summer and are not particularly warm in winter. They can also be very noisy during hail and rainstorms, upsetting the occupants.

Qualities of a good stable

There must not be any draughts in a stable, but plenty of fresh air is important. I agree with owners who never shut the top of their stable doors even in the coldest weather, providing their horses are properly rugged up.

The importance of adequate ventilation cannot be over-emphasized, because

Right: Stable doors should be wide and have plenty of headroom for the horse to look out. A metal covering along the top of the bottom door prevents the horse from chewing the wood. Proper stable bolts will be necessary along with a 'kick catch' at the bottom, to keep the occupants safely inside.

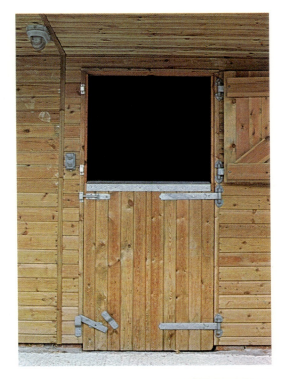

Below: The top part of the stable door should hinge outwards and fasten against the wall. Most of the time, it can be left open day and night, because horses need fresh air and cannot be kept fit in a stuffy stable.

horses, like human beings, continuously use up oxygen from the air and replace it with carbon dioxide as they breathe. When this is mixed with the rather acrid ammonia fumes produced by decomposing horse droppings, the result is not only very unpleasant to the horse, but can affect his wind and be injurious to his general welfare.

Windows are the best means of ventilation. They should preferably be situated above the animal's head, and must be barred or covered with wire mesh, and hinged at the bottom, opening inwards. The glass needs to be kept clean to allow plenty of daylight into the box.

Doorways should be at least 2.5 metres (8 ft) in height, and wide enough for a fully-tacked-up horse to go in and out easily without damage to himself or the saddlery. The doors should open outwards in two parts, so that the top can be left open and the horse can look out and see what is going on.

Doors need to be fitted with proper stable bolts, with a 'kick catch' at the bottom. If necessary, a ring may have to be placed through the door catch to prevent animals with 'Houdini' tendencies from letting themselves out when a kick catch is not in place. The tops of the doors should be covered with some form of galvanized sheeting to protect them from being chewed.

Some of the older brick-built stables have loose boxes reached through a main entrance and passageway, that do not enable an animal to see out into the yard. These boxes have their advantages, particularly as far as draughts are concerned, but if there is a choice I much prefer the other type.

Light switches must be of the round safety variety and outside the stable, well away from a horse's reach. This is important: when light switches have been placed too near a doorway, I have had horses get their heads round to switch them on and off with their teeth. Apart from being disconcerting to other horses at night, this results in rather large electricity bills!

The lights themselves should be well out of reach and be protected by wire cages to stop wisps of hay or straw reaching hot light bulbs. Wiring must be heavy duty and beyond the reach of a horse's teeth. If in doubt, have any worn wiring replaced.

Choosing the stable fittings

Few stable fittings are necessary in practice, and the more a loose box is free of encumbrances the better. I dislike mangers because they are difficult to clean, and I prefer horses to eat from a bowl on the ground, which is a more natural position for them. The bowl can be removed when a horse has finished feeding, so that food is not left to go stale.

A tie ring for the haynet will be necessary if a horse is bedded down on straw. It should be high enough to keep the haynet away from the horse's feet when empty, but not so high that the hayseeds get into the horse's eyes. I prefer feeding hay in sections on the floor if shavings are being used. The ground is always the most natural position for a horse to eat from, and he will amuse himself long after his feed is finished looking for wisps of hay among the shavings.

A tie ring in the wall at breast level is useful, but I find a loop of string or strong twine, held firmly in place with a large staple, does just as well. It prevents a horse breaking his headcollar if he jerks backwards for any reason, because the string will break first. The string can easily be renewed.

The water supply

I prefer strong plastic water buckets to automatic water bowls, because they make it possible to tell exactly how much water a horse is drinking. If for any reason I do not want him to have any water – perhaps just before he is going hunting or across country – the buckets can be removed.

Buckets should be checked at least three times a day, or, better still, every time you go into the stable. Horses seem to dislike water that has been standing all night; every morning the water buckets should be emptied, rinsed and refilled. Once a week, the buckets will need a thorough scrubbing-out to get rid of the layer of slime that often develops on the inside walls.

The buckets need to be solid enough to stand up to heavy wear and tear without splitting, and have a capacity of at least 9 litres (2 gals). They should be placed in

A horse can learn to switch his stable light on and off with his nose!

the corner of the box away from any hay-net, but near to the door where they can easily be seen. Rubber or heavy plastic is best for buckets; galvanized iron is noisy when knocked, and dents easily when kicked.

Horses will not thrive unless they have a constant supply of good clean water. There are owners who like to provide water that is at the same temperature as the atmosphere by keeping a tank or tub in the yard and filling the water buckets from it.

Nature teaches horses to drink a little at a time; you need not be concerned that they will over-drink at any time, provided that they know clean water is always available. Do not take any notice of warnings that horses will drink too much when they come in hot from exercise and will gripe themselves, and that they must always drink before a feed rather than afterwards.

The reasoning behind this mistaken view is that water passes more rapidly through the front part of a horse's gut; if feed is there already, this part of the sensitive intestine can be stretched, causing discomfort and colic.

Such a thing might have occurred with vanners and other trade horses, who were kept in rows of stables and taken to drink at irregular times from a communal water trough. If, when a horse returned from work to the stable yard, there was a queue at the trough and the driver was tired, he sometimes unharnessed the horse and fed him before offering the unfortunate animal a drink. The thirsty animal would then gulp down large quantities of water, knowing that he was unlikely to get any more before morning; and digestive troubles would almost certainly result. Had there been water in his stall, the problem would not have arisen.

Salt licks
Most horses appreciate a lump of salt they can lick in the stable. Metal holders, just the right size to hold a standard rectangular block of salt, can be purchased from most saddlers and fodder merchants. They screw to the wall at about head high. I have never found a horse that liked the brown medicated variety of salt block; the plain white salt seems to be more popular. A supply of salt is not essential, but most horses have a natural craving for salt from time to time. That is why some will get pleasure from licking your hand if it is damp. They can also satisfy this need by eating earth when they are turned out; or salt can be mixed with their feed.

The two main elements of salt, sodium and chlorine, are vital to a horse's welfare, and fortunately both are usually contained in his food. After hard work, a horse loses salt through sweating, and that is when he may need an extra supply. Because his needs vary, a horse may ignore his salt lick for days or even weeks, and then suddenly start to demolish the whole block. Even if a horse does not use his lick every day, it should still be left in his box.

Choosing bedding
The type of bedding to be used depends on a number of considerations. Before the days of combine harvesters, good wheat straw was easy to get and usually free from dust and short stalks. That, unfortunately, is no longer the case. Most of the straw bales produced by modern methods contain a great deal of dust and chaff. I doubt if it matters much, once the husks have been through a combine harvester, whether wheat or barley straw is used; but for a long time, barley straw was looked upon as inferior, because people thought that the long barley hairs could irritate the sensitive skin of a well-bred animal. Oat straw was also avoided because, being rather sweet-tasting, it was more likely to be eaten.

Although a horse will not come to any harm from eating oat straw, it has little

Hay nets are more popular than racks because there is less likelihood of hay being wasted. The correct amount can be weighed out for each horse with the aid of a simple spring scale kept in the hay barn. Care should be taken to ensure that a hay net is securely tied at about the level of a horse's nose, so that he will not get hay seeds in his eyes when he eats, and the net will be out of harm's way when empty.

Unless straw is dust free and of good quality, other types of bedding are more satisfactory, and are usually quicker to deal with. Straw looks nicer, but it has the drawback of being also pleasant to eat. Some owners dislike having to muzzle a horse to prevent it eating its bedding; and covering the straw with disinfectant is not effective. There is little point, however, in trying to ration a horse's food if he eats his bedding.

nutritional value. And apart from filling the horse's stomach to no good purpose, there is the expense of replacing the bed each morning.

If wheat straw is used, it should be dry, free from mould and blackness, and light gold in colour. That, however, rarely seems to be the case nowadays.

Using shavings for bedding

Because of the dusty nature and generally poor quality of most straw bales, my own preference is for shavings. They are easy to skip out, and although some horses will nibble at them when they are fresh, before they have been mixed with the old bedding, they are not normally eaten. Consequently, their use enables the owner to know exactly how much roughage or fibre a horse is getting, because the horse will not add to the roughage he is given by eating his straw bedding when he has finished his hay and still feels hungry. This is particularly important if a horse is expected to do fast work and be fit to race or compete in Horse Trials.

If shavings are used, it is important to ensure that they are free of any bits of wood and that they are not dusty. A horse can develop respiratory troubles through breathing in dust, particularly when he lies down. Saw mills supplying shavings differ in the quality they sell, and it is worth while checking with other owners. Problems with dusty shavings usually only arise when the sweepings from the saw mill floor are used. Shavings bought by the sack are easier to handle than those bought by the bale.

Before shavings are laid down, any stable drains should be covered to prevent them becoming blocked, and to make sure that a good depth of shavings can be maintained. After a few weeks, the bottom layer will become quite hard. Provided that droppings are skipped out regularly, wet shavings are removed, and the bed is topped up each day, a box with shavings should last for about six months before there is any need for the whole bed to be dug out and replaced.

Other types of bedding

Various other forms of bedding can also be used. These include peat moss, which is expensive and messy; sawdust, which tends to heat up as soon as it becomes soiled or damp; and shredded paper, which never seems satisfactory. In some stables, even dead leaves or dry bracken fern are used. Leaves are cheap but they quickly become soggy and bad for a horse's feet; and dry bracken can make a horse ill if it is eaten in any quantity.

The deciding factor in the choice of bedding may, however, eventually be the behaviour or allergies of the horse, and the availability and price of the types an owner is prepared to use. If you do plan to use straw, check that your horse is not allergic to it in the same way that some horses are allergic to hay and develop a chronic cough and nasal discharge rather like hay fever.

Stable equipment

The equipment needed in a stable yard will depend on the type and variety of bedding used. A good-sized wheelbarrow, a shovel and a bristle broom are essential, and so is a skip, which need only be a large plastic bowl. If straw is being used, a four-pronged dung fork is preferable to a pitchfork. A good thick pair of rubber gloves and a metal rake makes skipping out much easier with other types of bedding.

The tack room will obviously need enough saddle racks and bridle cups to cope with whatever saddlery you require. You will also need a large vermin-proof box in which to store unused rugs and blankets, and somewhere to keep the various other essentials, such as boots, bandages and cleaning materials.

The fodder store, which should be near the fresh-water supply, will need vermin-proof containers for such concentrates as bran and oats. But large plastic dustbins are quite effective and much cheaper than lined feed bins.

Because all foodstuff is expensive, it is important to prevent waste. This can be caused either by damage from the weather or by vermin. Rats and mice are quick to detect food left lying about in a fodder store, and also foul any other food they find.

The old saying 'a place for everything and everything in its place', is a good basic rule for good stable management. Cleanliness, tidiness and punctuality are all matters of habit; and they play an important part in the smooth running of an efficient stable yard.

Every stable should have a selection of implements for use in mucking out the boxes and keeping the stable yard clean. These could include a stiff yard brush, a rake, a shovel, a lighter brush and water buckets. They should be stored carefully where they can always be found.

4: The stable yard

Whether you are keeping one horse for your own pleasure, or a string of race-horses or show jumpers for other people, the principles of good stable management are the same. There are always too many jobs that have to be done, and they certainly will not get done properly if time has to be wasted looking for items that have been lost, or have been left in the wrong place.

Cleanliness is the first essential, whether the stable is new or, perhaps, an old converted cattle shed. A horse consumes large quantities of food, mostly in the form of hay or grass, and drinks large quantities of water: the result is that he produces substantial amounts of dung and urine which need to be dealt with regularly.

Deep litter systems, where the soiled bedding is left to build up gradually, with just a thick layer of new straw or shavings placed on top each day, are not really satisfactory. Although the bed is warm, it can get too hot and cause foot problems.

Caring for the muck heap

Finding a suitable place to put the large quantities of manure produced by even one horse, let alone a stableful, usually presents quite a problem. But it is essential to be able to clear the muck heap regularly not only because of the smell and the flies, but also because the warmth of the muck heap will almost certainly encourage vermin in the winter.

The heap must be well clear of buildings whose walls and foundations can also be damaged by the moisture. The ideal site is a sufficiently large piece of dry ground that a wheelbarrow can reach without getting

A clean and tidy stable yard not only looks well but also helps efficiency. There should be 'a place for everything and everything in it's place'. Stable hygiene is important, too, and stable yards need to be washed down and disinfected regularly. If cleaning the yard is made part of the stable routine, the job will not take long to do, and there will be much less likelihood of infection.

Keeping a muck heap trimmed and tidy is quite an art. When there is a large stable of horses, the manure heap can quickly become very unsightly unless it is managed properly. The manure should be encouraged to rot as quickly as possible so that it becomes useful as fertilizer. It will be of value not only for the household garden, but also to market gardeners who can then be persuaded to come and take it away. The top of the heap should be kept flat so that rainwater soaks down through the manure and helps with the rotting process. If the manure is allowed to develop into a mound, the water runs away down the sides and does not have the desired effect.

bogged down in wet weather, and which a tractor and trailer can get to easily.

Well-rotted horse manure is a useful garden fertilizer and worth maintaining in a proper stack. A three-sided frame made out of vertical sheets of corrugated iron nailed to posts about 1 metre (3 ft) in height is quite adequate. Or a better-looking version can be made with thick wooden planks. Really smart stables have manure heaps with surrounds made of cement blocks or even bricks. Cement-block or brick walls need to be carefully built, however, because rotted-down manure, apart from generating a considerable amount of heat, is also very heavy. Insecure walls can easily break down.

Manure should be stacked in a heap with a flat top and vertical sides that can be kept trimmed and tidy. Each wheelbarrow load should be spread evenly on the top of the heap and levelled off.

Water is essential for the rotting process, and the flat top enables rainwater to soak into the heap instead of running down the sides as it would do on a mound. Some form of composting agent, such as potassium nitrate, provides additional help to the rotting process.

Straw manure is obviously best for the garden in its natural state. But if shavings can be burnt slowly and continuously, the usefulness of the manure will be improved; vermin will be kept away, and the heap will be prevented from getting too large.

Caring for fodder

Hay that is kept badly will become damp and mouldy. This is not only wasteful, but, if fed to a horse, is likely to cause colic. It should be stored in a dry building, out of reach of animals and away from the elements. The hay store may be open sided provided that it is safe from drifting snow, which will lie on the top and soak down through the stack, ruining each bale it comes into contact with. If rain can reach the bales too easily, the outside layer will also be wasted because horses will not want to eat the affected hay.

Bales should be stacked in such a way that air can circulate freely. If the floor shows any signs of damp (and remember

Hay is very expensive and needs to be looked after and not wasted. It should be stacked in such a way that air can circulate freely. If an open sided barn is used, it is important to ensure that snow cannot drift up on top and penetrate down through the stack. Damp and mouldy hay can cause colic and should never be used.

that new concrete often weeps) a bottom layer of straw will be needed. Straw is cheaper than hay; but if none is available, last year's old bales of hay can be used, if they are dry and not too mouldy.

If straw is needed for bedding, it can be stacked alongside the hay. Provided that the necessary storage space is available, a winter's supply of hay and straw can be purchased straight from the fields when the price is relatively low.

Never waste money on bad, soft hay as there is no nourishment in it. It is far better for the horse, and for your bank balance, to buy good hard hay and feed it in smaller quantities.

Good forage can be recognized by using all the senses. It should be hard and crisp, should look bright, and should smell sweet. Remember the old grooms' saying: 'Oats must rattle, hay must crackle, and bran should be floury and have a good taste.' If you follow that maxim and store food well, there is no need for waste, and

less likelihood of horses developing digestive ailments.

The hay store must always be kept tidy. Hay and straw should be used one bale at a time, otherwise there will be many half-used bales loose on the floor getting dirty and, eventually, being wasted. A large, sharp pair of scissors should be hung on a handy nail to cut the baler twine, which can then be rolled up and kept in a sack.

You will also need a spring balance to check the weight of the haynets and how much a horse is getting. Buy a balance capable of weighing up to 10kgs (20lb) with reasonable accuracy. Corn scoops, spare water buckets and feed bowls can all be kept in the fodder store.

Finally, do not hoard broken wheelbarrows, old brooms and headcollars, worn out dandy brushes and bottles containing unlabelled liquids. They only collect dust and make a yard look untidy. It is a hundred to one that you will never find a use for any of them.

5: Feeding

Grass is a natural food for horses and grazing in a field is the natural way for them to eat. A horse or pony living out all the year round can usually get all the nourishment he needs in summer from the grass available. But in winter, when the grass has stopped growing and has lost his grass and roughage in the form of hay

If an animal is expected to work, he will also need something extra in winter in the way of concentrates to give him energy and warmth. This is, however, an artificial form of feeding, and because a horse has quite a delicate digestive system which can easily be upset, care must be taken to ensure that these foods are fed correctly and in the right amounts.

A horse's eating habits differ considerably from those of his owner. Whereas human beings can cope with three or four large meals a day, a horse has a very small stomach for his size; and what is even more important, unlike a dog, his stomach will not stretch very much. If he bolts a big meal, he is likely to get colic.

That is why a horse will keep munching away quite contentedly when he is out in a field. His normal diet of grass also contains a high percentage of water, which, like the roughage, is essential to his well-being. But this does not mean that he can live without a further supply of clean water.

Concentrates must always be stored in vermin-proof bins. Those designed specifically for the purpose are, of course, ideal; but plastic dustbins are adequate and are much less expensive. It is important that all food offered to horses should be palatable and appetizing; and, as all feeds tend to deteriorate, they must not be allowed to become damp and musty.

How a horse digests food

Digestion obviously starts in the mouth with the chewing process, when the food is mixed with saliva before entering the stomach. There, it is subjected to the gastric juices before passing into the intestines for the final stage of digestion to take place.

The outlet to a horse's intestines is, however, placed in such a way that it begins to pass food through when the intestines are only about three-quarters full. As a result, while the animal is feeding, there is a constant flow of food in and out. The stomach is never entirely full, but never entirely empty either.

That is why the rule with stabled horses is 'feed little but often'. A horse should never be kept without food for more than four or five hours at a time, because if he is forced to wait too long between meals, he will become very hungry and bolt down his food in too dry a state, without sufficient mastication. The stomach will then become overloaded, because it will not be able to deal with the meal in the way nature intended, and the normal process of digestion will be affected. When that happens, the horse may just get a mild attack of indigestion and look out of sorts. But the upset can sometimes be much more serious, and acute colic can be fatal.

Some horses need more food than others even though they are expected to do the same amount of work. This variation must be taken into account when planning a horse's diet.

To feed a horse properly, it is important to understand the animal's natural way of life, how his digestion works, and how his food is utilized. Without this knowledge, an owner will never be able to develop the sense of judgement required to get the best from a horse by correct feeding.

How much to feed, and the type of food to give, is frequently a matter of trial and error. As with humans, what suits one horse does not always suit another.

Feeding a horse kept at grass

When an animal is at grass the situation is relatively simple. In the summer months, providing there is a constant supply of clean water, the main problem will probably be to ensure that a horse does not get too fat. Too much flesh is detrimental to health, and in the summer there are far too many cases of lameness and respiratory diseases caused by horses being galloped and jumped when they are out of condition. Horses are fundamentally lazy, and when they can get all the food they require with a minimum of time and effort, they are inclined to spend more time lying down or lazing in the shade, instead of walking round the field and getting exercise.

It is impossible to get a horse or pony into hard condition if he is fed only on hay and grass. Some form of concentrate will be needed, depending on how much work he is expected to do.

A good method is to stable a horse for two or three hours before he is ridden. Then when he returns from the ride, he can be given a feed and turned out. Never feed before exercise. Always allow at least an hour's interval, and if you have to ride a horse or pony straight from the field, try to spend the first 45 minutes walking because he may have been filling his stomach with grass before being caught. A little care and understanding will save money in veterinary bills.

A sudden change of diet should be avoided, but when the grass starts to get rather lush in spring it may be necessary to alter the amount and type of supplementary feeding. Otherwise, the horse or pony may put on too much weight. If an animal is looking well, seems to have plenty of energy, is alert, takes an interest in everything going on around him, and has a shining coat, even in winter, he is probably being well fed and is receiving the correct amount of concentrates.

If, however, he is thin and in poor condition with his coat stark and his ribs

Mares and foals are happier turned out in well-fenced pastures where they can be in their more natural state. The grazing, however, must not be too lush, and they will need shelter and a good supply of clean water. In winter, they will require regular feeds of hay and proteins. Horses turned out must never be left for long periods without attention.

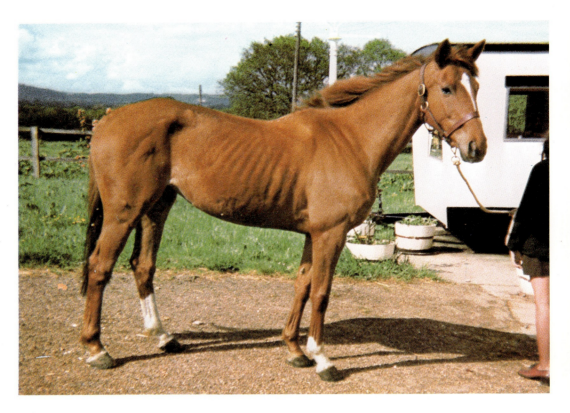

visible, and he tends to stand 'tucked up' with his head down and looking miserable, then action will be needed. Do not be fooled by a thick winter coat, which can often hide a very thin frame.

The horse may have lost condition through not getting enough of the right type of food. If he is in a field with other animals, they may be worrying him and preventing him from having his fair share.

There may however be other reasons. The obvious one is that he is ill and needs urgent veterinary attention. More likely, he is suffering from worms, which are taking all the goodness from the food he eats. Or perhaps his teeth have become pointed and sharp so that he cannot use them for chewing his food. If they are very sharp they can also cut his mouth.

If that is the case, a veterinary surgeon can rasp the horse's teeth smooth again quite easily and painlessly. Indeed, there are some people who spend their whole

Top: A Thoroughbred mare that was obviously suffering badly from malnutrition and worms at the time she came into the hands of a new owner. Tests were carried out to ensure that the right worm powders were used, and she was given four meals of concentrates a day and as much hay as she wanted. Her coat lost its dull look; her neck began to build up; and as she began to put on weight her tail carriage improved.

Right: No lasting damage had been done, and within six weeks the mare's condition had improved greatly. Within two months, she was jumping clear rounds in foxhunter show jumping competitions and taking part in the Pony Club show jumping championships. This horse is a splendid example of how correct care can bring an animal back to condition.

time visiting stables as 'horse dentists', dealing with tooth problems. The teeth of a horse or pony need attention at least once a year after they are fully grown.

Worms must also be dealt with. Excellent worm powders are available that can be mixed with a feed, or wormers in liquid form can be squirted down the horse's throat with a syringe. A veterinary surgeon will always advise on which form to use. Worming needs to be done regularly: at least three times a year for a horse at grass, and four times a year for a stabled animal.

Feeding a stable-kept horse

When a horse is kept under less natural conditions in a stable, the amount of food he is given will depend on his size and the work he is expected to do. I feel that even a rough daily guide may be misleading, because horses' requirements can differ greatly and finding the best bal-

anced diet may take time. If you are not sure of the best amount to start with, check with the horse's previous owner as to how much he was feeding. If this is not possible, your veterinary surgeon will, no doubt, be willing to advise you. In time, you will be able to judge for yourself by the way a horse or pony looks and behaves.

Larger horses doing hard work, such as hunting, show jumping or competing in Horse Trials, can have a higher proportion of such feedstuffs as oats, bruised barley and horse nuts in each feed.

Oats should never be fed to small ponies or horses in light work. The daily ration of concentrates should be split into two, three or four feeds a day, depending on the time available for feeding and looking after the horse. But most horses in light work will require at least half the concentrates to be in the form of bran, chaff and vegetable foods like carrots.

Because horses are creatures of habit,

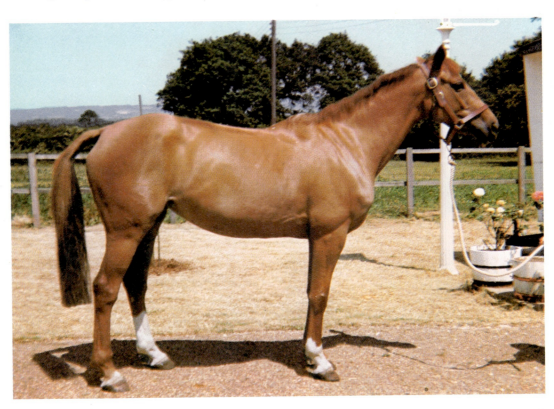

they prefer to be fed at the same time each day. Although feed times may have to be adjusted to suit an owner's working hours, or perhaps the timing of a particular competition, it is important to keep to a timetable as far as possible.

For a stabled horse getting three feeds a day, morning, noon and night are the best times to feed, according to his periods of exercising or schooling. A further feed may be given in the late afternoon.

Horses will never thrive on poor quality or stale food; it may even cause harm. Mouldy hay, for example, can cause respiratory problems as well as colic. It may be cheaper to buy, but will prove to be very much more expensive in the long run.

Some owners like their stabled horses to have all the hay they can eat. I prefer to feed a small section of hay with the early feed at least two hours before the horses are due to be worked. Hay can be given again after morning exercise, and they can have the remainder of their ration in the evening after the final feed of the day.

Horses should be left alone when they are eating to enjoy their food without interruption. Never throw food in to them. Think of your own reaction if someone threw a plate of food in front of you without a word. Unless you were very hungry, and it was particularly tasty, you would probably refuse to eat it. Far better to put a horse's feed before him with an encouraging word and a pat. Your horses are more likely to turn out to be 'good doers' if you do.

Always dampen food concentrates. This will not only make them less likely to be spilt, but also prevent dust from the food getting into the horse's lungs.

Feeding hay

I prefer feeding hay from the floor if a horse is kept on shavings, and from a haynet if he is on straw. Outside, however, it is a good idea to provide a good strong hay rack that will not tip over. It will prevent the hay from getting trampled underfoot, particularly in wet weather. Some owners tie a haynet to the branch of a tree or on a fence. This is a dangerous practice, because as the haynet becomes empty it drops nearer the ground and can easily get entangled in a horse's legs. The result can be disastrous. I have heard of ponies that have had to be put down after such an occurrence, because the more they struggled to free themselves the more the twine cut into their legs until it almost severed their fetlocks. It is not a risk worth taking.

Finding good quality food is not always easy, but it pays to search around for the best source of supply. *Seed hay* is best for horses at grass because it has more food value, is harder than meadow hay, and contains mostly rye grass and clover. It should be fairly light in colour, with a green hue and a pleasant smell. The clover should have plenty of leaf and flower, and the rye grass stalks should be bright.

Meadow hay is cut from old-established pasture, and should contain a variety of grasses in addition to clover. There should not be much weed; and although meadow hay is softer in texture than seed hay, the herbage should not be matted or have a woolly look. If it is in good condition, it should still have quite a lot of green about it, and retain that new-mown smell.

Hay is best cut in early summer before it loses quality. Look for plenty of leaf and flower, which will signify that it has been cut before the grasses have gone to seed and lost their nutritional value. Second crop hay is of little use to horses; and hay made after a storm of rain has washed mud onto the stalks is likely to be dusty. Mildewed and dusty hay irritates the lungs and is often the cause of broken wind.

Choosing oats

There is no better food for promoting energy and developing muscle on a horse than oats. There are varieties of colour

It is natural for a horse to eat his food from the floor, and when shavings are used for bedding it may be preferable to feed hay from the ground instead of from a rack or haynet. There is no chance of hay seeds getting into the eyes, and horses seem to enjoy nosing about for wisps of hay among the shavings. However, if straw is used in place of shavings, feeding from the floor is not a good idea, because it invites a horse to eat his bedding.

including black, white and grey. The colour does not matter, however, provided that the grains are short and plump, and that there are not too many husks. Good oats should weigh about 1 kilogramme to 2 litres (40 lb to the bushel). If it weighs less it will probably have too many husks. The grains should be heavy to handle, and should make a rustling noise as they fall through the fingers. Remember that oats must always be dry and free from odour. In a wet harvest, when the oats often have to be kiln dried, they get a peculiar smell that horses dislike. Grain should not be given to horses until it is at least a year old.

Some people prefer to buy whole oats, and have them crushed before they are delivered so that they can see their quality – particularly as oats that have been over-pulped are sometimes rather

dusty. It is not harmful to feed whole oats, but they are inclined to pass through a horse without being properly digested. Unfortunately, in times of shortage and high labour costs, few corn merchants are prepared to provide much choice. It is however worth trying to find a merchant who provides the best quality.

Choosing barley

Barley should weigh about 2 kilogrammes to 3 litres (56 lb to the bushel), and may be judged in a similar way to oats. It should always be fed bruised because it is indigestible if the husks are not cracked. Barley should also be boiled and allowed to soak for a few hours before being fed, because during the boiling process the grains swell to about twice their dry volume and become easy to digest. Boiled barley is normally mixed with bran and

43

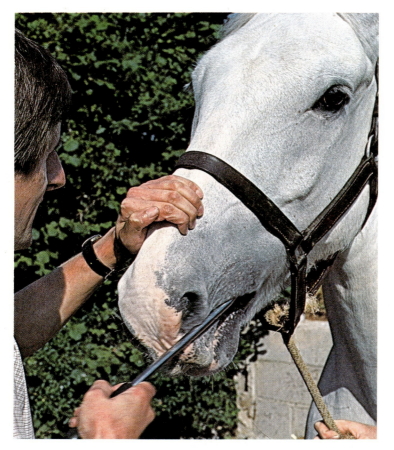

other concentrates, and can help improve the condition of a horse which has been off colour. Oats may also be boiled in the same way, to make them more digestible for a horse who has been ill or out of sorts.

Other foodstuffs

Another nutritious food for putting weight on a horse or pony is *flaked maize*, which is made by flaking and drying cooked maize. But because it tends to be lighter than oats or barley, it should be fed sparingly, and always with roughage such as bran or chaff.

Beans are sometimes given to horses. But they should only be fed in small quantities to horses who use up a great deal of energy by being worked hard or to horses who are living out in very cold weather and need warmth. Beans, whether whole or split, should always be introduced into a diet slowly. Remember the saying 'full of beans'; beans can give a horse an excessive amount of energy.

The minced pulp of *sugar beet* is another useful form of animal feed. As it is marketed dried, it must be soaked overnight in a bucket of water to allow the beet to swell fully. Otherwise the swelling process would take place in a horse's stomach and cause colic. Sugar beet is a useful source of energy and can be used to supplement, or even partially replace, a ration of corn or horse nuts.

Molassine meal, made as a by-product of sugar refining, is a black, treacly-smelling substance that may be fed as a supplement to other concentrates. Because it tastes sweet, horses usually like it, so it is a useful addition to the feeds of any animals who tend to be rather faddy eaters.

Horse nuts or cubes have now become part of the staple diet in many stables, and provide minerals that might otherwise be lacking. There are various types of nuts that can be fed in place of oats or barley, or in conjunction with other concentrates. They must, however, always be stored in a dry place and kept in good condition. The best-known brands are good; but they can differ in quality because sometimes ingredients have to be changed if there is a shortage of any particular foodstuff. When this happens, there may also be a change

in colour, and the alteration then becomes evident.

Linseed is the small brown seed of the flax plant, and is claimed by many to put a shine on a horse's coat and improve condition, especially in cold weather. I have yet to be really convinced of this. Linseed must always be fed cooked because it is poisonous to horses in its uncooked state. About 200 grams (6oz) of linseed for each horse should be placed in an old saucepan kept for the purpose, and covered with water, which should be brought to the boil and kept boiling for 15 minutes. The heat should then be reduced, and the linseed left to simmer gently for a further six hours, with more water being added if necessary. When the mixture is allowed to cool, it will turn into a rather

A young owner learning how to mix a feed and to tell whether the concentrates are in good condition. Good feeding is an art, and a horseman is never too young to learn how to get the best results by careful feeding.

messy-looking jelly, which most horses and ponies enjoy, particularly when it is fed with the cooked linseed and bran as a warm mash. If a number of horses are being kept, a small boiler can be used instead of a saucepan.

How to feed bran

Bran is a by-product of the milling of wheat, and broad bran is the fibrous outer husk in the form of large flakes. Fine bran is all right for pet rabbits and guinea pigs, being dusty is not good for horses.

Whatever the size of the flake, bran should always smell sweet, and not be lumpy or show any sign of sourness or mould. Although it has some nutritive value, its real use is as roughage or a mild laxative, and it should always be fed dampened.

Bran on its own makes an excellent mash, and is a very useful diet for a sick horse or one convalescing. A bran mash

A bran mash is simple to make and an excellent feed for a sick or tired horse. It cannot be made in a rush, but should be prepared about an hour before feed time and left to cool. The temperature is tested with the elbow to gauge when the mash is ready.

should always be fed if a horse is tired after a hard day's work, particularly after hunting, and should in any case be given to every stabled horse at least once a week as an evening meal.

The mash is made by putting a full measure of bran and a tablespoon of salt into a bucket, and saturating it with boiling water. After being stirred thoroughly, preferably with a big wooden spoon or round piece of wood, the bucket should then be covered with a cloth, or a piece of sacking, and the mixture left to soak and cool.

To make certain that it is cool enough to feed, dip your elbow in the mash. If you can do so without any feeling of discomfort, the mash is ready. It will usually take an hour or so to cool sufficiently; but stir well before you test the temperature, because pockets of scalding bran sometimes remain in the bottom of the bucket when the rest seems ready to feed. To make the mash a little more tempting, a few oats may be sprinkled on top.

Giving variety

Variety in a diet is important, because

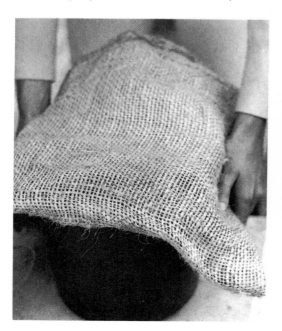

46

horses do not like eating the same food every day. A change can be provided by adding cleaned and cooked parings of such vegetables as potatoes, swedes, turnips, parsnips or perhaps kale. Raw carrots and apples, which have been carefully cut lengthways into fingers to avoid the risk of a horse choking, make excellent additions to a diet. And if you want to conceal medicines in a feed, add a little black treacle; this is not only nutritious but is looked upon by most horses as a real treat.

Chaff, which is usually a mixture of hay and good-quality oat straw cut into short lengths, is fine roughage. When mixed with a feed, it will make a horse thoroughly masticate his food. It must never be dusty; and if possible it is as well to have your own chaff cutter, because you cannot always be sure that the chaff you buy has not been made from sweepings.

Horses must always have a constant supply of fresh water, and the bucket should be placed near the door where it can be seen. This reminds the owner that it needs refilling.

6: Tack and the tack room

The tack room must be dry, warm and, above all, secure: saddlery has become very expensive and is a profitable target for thieves. There should be room to hang up all the clean saddles and bridles. Good quality leather remains strong and supple for many years, provided that it is looked after properly and stored away carefully when not in use. Rugs, boots and bandages should also be kept clean and in good repair, and stored in a dry place.

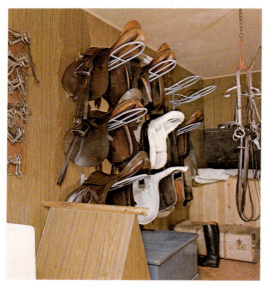

A well-kept tack room, emitting that lovely smell of freshly cleaned leather, is a joy to own and a pleasure to work in. There is also the added incentive to proper management of the tack room that as all saddlery is expensive and will deteriorate if left untreated, it needs to be looked after properly. Air temperature and humidity are important.

Leather has two sides, a grain and a flesh side. During the process of curing, great care is taken to conserve the natural fat and oil in the hide. Heat, sweat, water, grease and dirt reduce the fat content, making the leather dry and stiff. Hard leather is not only brittle, it is very uncomfortable for a horse. This means that every time a saddle, bridle or other item of tack is used, the dirt must be removed and the fat replaced, otherwise the saddlery will soon perish and become unsafe.

The surface of leather, the grain side, is waterproofed, and the pores are closed. They are left open, however, on the flesh side to allow the leather to absorb nourishment. It is this side which needs the greatest care during cleaning.

How to clean tack
Tack should be taken completely to pieces for cleaning. Then a sponge, wrung out in a bucket of tepid water, can be used to remove every particle of dirt and sweat. After the leather has been allowed to dry, a good leather dressing, such as saddle soap, should be applied, particularly to the flesh side, and rubbed in well. This will help to keep the leather supple and prevent it from going as stiff as a board when it gets wet. It will also help to preserve the stitching.

Cleaning tack can be quite a pleasant and rewarding task, particularly in summer when it can be done out of doors. All that is needed is a saddle horse and some buckets of clean water.

Saddlery that has a nasty, dark, thick coating of soap, scurf, grease, mud and grit has obviously not been cleaned correctly. Properly treated leather should have a deep sheen rather than a high polish.

Tack must be kept in a dry place away from artificial heat, which dries out the natural oils. Air temperature and humidity greatly affect leather, because when it gets too hot it becomes brittle, and in a cold, damp atmosphere it absorbs water and feels nasty and sodden. A warmish, damp atmosphere will produce large quantities of mould, a sure indication that the saddlery should be kept elsewhere.

Good quality, well-cared-for leather rarely breaks and will remain strong and supple for many years. Even so, stitching must be kept under constant scrutiny, because all stitching rots in time, however good the conditions. Do not forget that sound leather can be re-stitched if need be. You will soon learn the places to look for. Straps tend to give first at the holes, and that is why buckles should be undone during cleaning, so that any worn stitching can be detected more easily. Stirrup leathers, in particular, wear badly at the holes, and should be changed over frequently. If this is not done, the near-side

leather, which takes the rider's weight when mounting, will become longer than the other. A good saddler can always take leathers up at the buckle end.

Reins, girths and stirrup leathers, in particular, have to withstand considerable strain from time to time, and need to be inspected regularly. The girth straps on the saddle and their fixings must also be watched for wear; and buckle guards that fit over the girth buckles to prevent them wearing a hole in the saddle flap should always be used.

Metal items of saddlery (such as bits, stirrup irons and buckles) must be wiped clean and polished with a dry rag. The tongues of buckles need frequent oiling to facilitate free movement.

Choosing tack

Pure nickel stirrups and bits are cheap, but they are unreliable and are best avoided. A nickel stirrup may bend and trap a rider's foot if a horse falls. Nickel mixtures are more expensive, but the extra cost is money well spent. My own preference is for stainless steel, which is smart and dependable.

Leather girths are recommended except for cross-country riding, when two single webbing girths with elastic insets are more effective. The webbing can be cleaned with a dandy brush. If a nylon-string girth is used, it can be washed and left to dry overnight.

Felt or sheepskin numnahs can be brushed. But saddle cloths, saddle blankets, wither pads and foam rubber numnahs need to be washed.

Bits

Inexperienced riders, when they have difficulty in controlling a horse, often jump to the conclusion that a more severe bit is the obvious answer to their problem. Nothing could be further from the truth, because a horse's usual reaction to pain is to pull harder. In an effort to ease the pain and evade the action of the bit, he will either cross his jaw, throw up his head, lean on the bit or put his tongue over it.

In fact, a horse who tends to take a rather strong hold may go more kindly in a snaffle because it gives him less discomfort. It is seldom possible to hit on the most suitable bit for a horse straight away. More often, it is a matter of trial and error until the right bit is found. You can then decide whether some form of martingale would also help the situation.

Not only must the correct type of bit be found, but the one chosen must be the correct width for the particular horse's mouth; otherwise the action will be impaired. The bridle should be adjusted until the bit just touches the corners of the mouth without wrinkling or drawing them up. In the case of a double bridle, the snaffle should touch the corners, with the bit lying just below it. The curb chain can be adjusted by letting it hang loose from the off-side hook, and then twisting it to the right until all the links are smooth. Give the smooth chain another half turn to the right, and then place it on the near-side hook at the length you require. The chain will then lie flat against the chin groove when pressure is put on the reins. If the links are not flat, they will chafe the jaw bone, causing considerable pain. The

Right: The double bridle requires two reins and its action is far more complicated. It consists of a bradoon or snaffle bit and a curb bit. The severity will depend on the length of cheek of the curb bit and the adjustment of the curb chain.

Far right: The Pelham is really trying to have the same action as a double bridle but with only one bit. A curb chain is used, but the shape of the mouthpiece can vary considerably. Some riders feel it is a compromise which is rarely satisfactory, but it is a very helpful bit for younger riders and novices particularly as the two reins can be dispensed with if short leather straps are used to join the top and bottom rings on each side and a single rein fastened round each leather. Its action is then rather similar to the more popular Kimblewick.

curb should be used with a chin strap to prevent it from riding up, and should come into action when the cheeks of the bit are drawn back to an angle of 45 degrees. When the reins are slack, there should be adequate room for three fingers to pass between the curb chain and the jaw bone.

If you want to use a double bridle and are unsure which type to choose, start by trying one consisting of a Weymouth bit with a sliding mouthpiece and a short check, used in conjunction with a plain snaffle. This combination will encourage a horse to play with the bit more, and relax his bottom jaw in response to the rein.

There are also various types of Pelham bits used in conjunction with a curb which the majority of horses take to quite kindly. The most popular is the vulcanite or rubber-mouth Pelham, the Scamperdale and the Kimblewick. The last is ideal for children because it only requires a single rein. Short leather straps can also be

Above: The plain eggbut snaffle with a jointed mouthpiece, used here with an ordinary bridle with grakle noseband. The eggbut type is becoming more in use because the bit rings are fixed and less likely to pinch the sides of the horse's mouth. The mildest form of snaffle is the rubber mullen mouth variety. Various type of noseband can be used with the snaffle bit, but the most popular is the cavesson which can be used with a standing martingale.

buckled from the upper to the lower loops on each side of the other Pelham bits to allow a single rein to be used instead of the usual two.

A Hackamore, which is best known form of single rein bitless bridle, is always a useful item in any tack room in case a horse needs exercise but is unable to wear a bit through injury. It consists of two long metal cheeks, curved to embrace the nose by means of leather attachments which act on the chin and cartilage of the nose. This bridle is of Mexican origin and derives its name from the Spanish *jaquimi*, meaning *headstall*.

Great care should be taken not only in fitting the Hackamore, but also in the way it is used. If it is fitted incorrectly and is being used by a bad rider, it can cause great pain.

Choosing nosebands

There are many different nosebands to go with the various bits. The cavesson, which is buckled above the bit and under

the cheekpieces of the bridle, has become the most common. It needs to be adjusted until it is buckled to about two fingers' width below the horse's cheekbone, and is loose enough to admit two fingers comfortably between noseband and jaw.

The drop noseband is frequently used to prevent a horse evading control by opening his mouth or crossing his jaws. Very often, when a horse cannot be held satisfactorily in a snaffle, a drop noseband will help. The bottom strap of the drop noseband buckles below the bit. But the front of the noseband must be high enough not to interfere with the soft part of the horse's nose, or it will impede breathing and cause discomfort. It need not be buckled tightly, because its effect does not depend primarily on the animal being unable to open his mouth.

Remember, however, that a horse's nose is extremely sensitive, and on no account should a standing martingale be attached to a drop noseband, or it will cause severe pain when a horse throws his head up. If a standing martingale is necessary, a flash noseband can be used which is similar in action to a drop noseband. A grakle noseband, made popular by show jumpers, is another form of double noseband which is designed for a horse that 'yaws', reaches for the bit with his mouth open, or swings his head. It is named after the winner of the 1931 Grand National, who first wore one.

Choosing and using a martingale

Good hands go a long way towards eliminating the need for any type of martingale, with the probable exception of the Irish martingale or Irish rings. This is a short leather strap with a ring at each end through which the reins are passed; it is used mostly in racing to prevent the reins from going over a horse's head in the event of a fall.

Martingales are, however, popular with many riders, and a standing martingale running from the girth to noseband will help to control a confirmed 'stargazer'.

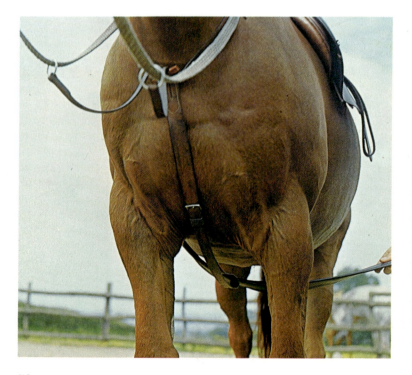

The running martingale is held in place by the girth at one end, and has rings through which the reins are passed. It is correctly adjusted when the rings are in line with the withers. When the horse raises his head beyond the limit allowed by the martingale, there is a downward pull on the bit; in the case of a snaffle, the pull is more onto the bars and away from the corners of the mouth. The tighter the martingale, the greater is the rider's control.

When a standing martingale is adjusted in such a way that a horse can raise his muzzle to the level of his withers, but no higher, it will not impede normal movement or prevent a horse extending himself properly when jumping.

A running martingale, which is firmly fixed only at the girth, and which allows much more freedom of movement, is usually considered more suitable for jumping. It is the only type allowed in some show-jumping competitions.

Choosing a saddle

The type and shape of a saddle is a matter of personal taste and comfort and how the horse is used. It must however fit correctly, or the horse's movement will be affected, and saddle sores and other ailments will result.

All saddles are built on a frame known as a *tree*, which determines the shape, size and fit of each saddle, and which is usually made in three widths to fit narrow, medium and wide horses. Because riders can vary so much in height, the seat of the saddle is also made in different lengths.

When buying a saddle, it is necessary to make sure that the tree is the correct width for the horse, and that the seat is the right length for its rider. A saddle is the most expensive of all items of saddlery, and must be right.

Saddles that are too narrow will pinch a horse's withers, and those that are too wide will move about too much and cause galling. Trees that are the wrong size cannot be altered successfully, and it is never worth attempting to do so.

A seat that is too short will throw the rider's weight into the cantle of the saddle,

Unless a saddle fits correctly the performance of the horse will be affected, and he will be liable to various ailments that can, in time, make him impossible to ride. Correct fit at the withers is important if pinching and galling are to be avoided.

and one too long will set the rider too far forward. Either way will lead to a feeling of insecurity.

When the rider is mounted there should always be at least two fingers' width clearance between the top of the horse's withers and the underside of the pommel. Back problems are inevitable for the horse if the cantle at the back of the saddle presses down onto his spine. A horse with a particularly high and narrow wither usually requires a saddle with a cut-back head – a type sometimes known as an 'open pommel' saddle. Badly fitting saddles are the cause of much back trouble in horses, and frequently result in an animal starting to buck. They can also cause unevenness in a horse's stride.

7: Grooming and clipping

Daily grooming is essential for the stabled horse, and the grooming kit should always be kept together in a special bag or box. When horses are denied the opportunity to exercise and roll at will, their skin and feet suffer unless they get regular attention. It must be remembered that the skin is as vital to the health of a horse as his heart or his lungs, and it must not be neglected. The saying 'no foot, no horse' is very true.

Horses at grass can be made to look very smart during the summer, but in winter, when they roll in the mud and use their caked covering of mud as protection against the weather, they are impossible to keep really clean. They also need the natural grease in their coats as a further protection, and thorough grooming in winter is not good for them. Before a horse is ridden, however, a dandy brush or a rubber curry comb should be used to take away most of the mud, particularly in the areas covered by the saddle and

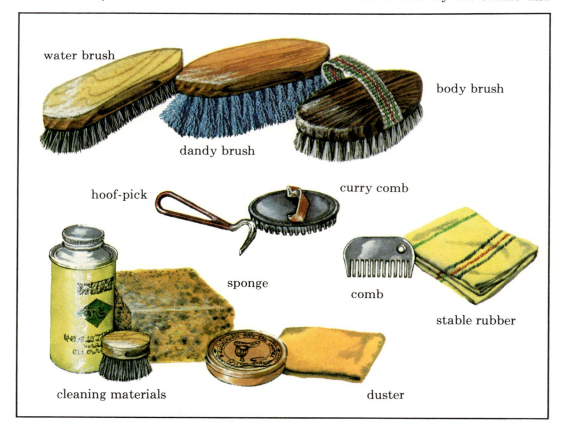

water brush

body brush

dandy brush

curry comb

hoof-pick

sponge

comb

stable rubber

cleaning materials

duster

Grooming should start with the horse's feet. Each foot should be picked up in turn and any dirt or stones removed with the point of the hoof pick, working downwards from the heel towards the toe. It is important to use the pick in this direction because its sharp tip may otherwise penetrate the soft parts of the frog. The cleft of the frog should also be cleaned out and any signs of thrush dealt with. Thrush results from inflammation of the glands of the sensitive frog, and is easily recognized by its distinctive smell. The shoe should then be tapped to see that it is secure, and the fingers should be run round the clenches to check them.

The dandy brush is used to get rid of mud, sweat marks or caked dirt. Starting at the poll, it can be used in either hand in a to-and-fro motion, but care must be taken to avoid the more tender parts of the body. The area of the saddle, the belly, the points of the hocks, the fetlocks and the pasterns should all come in for special attention.
A rubber curry comb can be used instead of a dandy brush, particularly when horses come in from a field and are caked with mud.

bridle. The feet also have to be picked out regularly with a hoof pick in order to remove dirt and stones, and this really needs to be done at the start and finish of a ride.

During the summer, there is no reason why a horse at grass should not get the same grooming as one that is stabled. The reason for giving a horse a good daily grooming is not just to smarten him up. Grooming improves a horse's circulation and helps tone up his muscles, in addition to maintaining him in good condition and preventing disease.

A horse moults twice a year: in the spring, when a large quantity of hair is shed and the short, sleek summer coat is grown; and in autumn, when the short hairs are replaced by the longer and more greasy winter coat. When a horse is turned out and the weather is really cold, his hair will stand on end, increasing the layer of warm air trapped inside and improving the insulation against the cold. That is why once the coat is dry it is

Below: The body brush has short, close-set hairs, designed to reach right through the coat to the skin. It is used in conjunction with a metal curry comb. The body brush should be taken in the left hand, when working on the near side of the body with the curry comb in the right. The reverse is the case when working on the other side. The brush should be used in short circular strokes in the direction of the lay of the coat, and then cleaned every three or four strokes by drawing it smartly across the teeth of the curry comb.

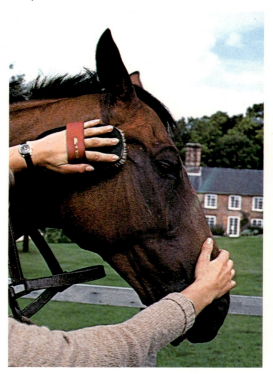

important to brush out any sweat marks, where the hairs have become stuck together, before turning an animal out after a ride; otherwise the hairs will not be able to stand up properly.

How to groom

Grooming should follow a routine that ensures that every part of the horse is dealt with in turn. Apart from the grooming kit, a bucket of water will be needed. The horse should be tied up on a short rack, and in sunny weather it is often more pleasant to groom outside, preferably somewhere in the shade.

Begin every time by picking out each foot in turn. Start at the heel and work the *hoof pick* towards the toe, taking care to clean the grooves on either side of the frog. Clear the cleft of the frog, and look for any signs of thrush.

When picking out, put the muck in a dung skip so that loose stones and dirt do not drop on to the stable floor, or in the stable yard. If they do, the horse will stand on them and get them back into his feet again.

After picking out, tap the shoes in turn to see that they are secure. Then run a finger round the clenches (the ends of the nails) to see that none are risen.

Beginning on the near side at the horse's poll, use the *dandy brush* in a to-and-fro motion and go all over the body to remove any caked dirt and sweat marks. Be careful, however, when brushing the loins or other tender parts.

The short, close-set hairs of the *body brush*, which is used next, are designed to reach through the coat to the skin. Except when being used on the mane and tail, the body brush should be worked mainly in short circular strokes in the direction of the lay of the coat. After every four or five strokes, the brush should be drawn across the teeth of a *curry comb* to remove grease and loose hairs. When full, the curry comb can be emptied by a gentle tap on the floor. For the horse's head to be brushed, the headcollar will have to be

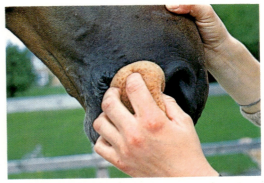

A soft, clean, sponge is required for wiping clean the eyes (above). This should be done carefully, sponging away from the corners and the eyelids. The sponge should then be wrung out and used to clean the area of the muzzle, including the lips and the inside and outside of the nostrils (above right). The dock area comes next (right). Most people prefer to keep a sponge especially for that purpose, but if the same sponge is being used it must again be rinsed. The tail is lifted and the sponge used to clean the area under the tail and then the dock.

dropped and the headstrap fastened temporarily round the neck. This brushing must be done gently, using the free hand to steady the head. Always use a body brush on the tail; never use a dandy brush, which will only remove and break the hairs, making the tail appear thin and unsightly.

A *wisp* (a pad made of woven hay) is then used to massage, develop and harden the muscles, and to give a shine to the coat by squeezing oil from the glands in the skin. Dampen the wisp slightly and bring it down with a bang in the direction of the lay of the coat. Give special attention to the parts where the muscles are hard and flat, but avoid all bony prominences and the tender region of the loins. If you are unable to make a suitable wisp, a round leather pad sold by many saddlers can be used to similar effect.

Next dampen a sponge in the bucket of water and sponge the eyes, working away from the corners and around the eyelids. Wring out the sponge and wipe the muzzle area, including the lips and the inside and outside of the nostrils. After washing out the sponge once more, lift the tail as high as possible with one hand and clean the whole of the dock region, including the under surface of the tail. Horses appreciate the refreshing effect of this sponging so long as it is done carefully. Some people prefer to keep a sponge for use only on the dock area.

A *water brush* dipped in the water is then applied flat to the mane, brushing the hairs from the roots downwards. The water brush can also be used to wash the feet; but the thumb of the hand holding the hoof should be pressed well down into the hollow of the heel, to prevent any water from becoming lodged there. When the hoof is dry, it can be treated with *hoof oil*, using a small paint brush. This not only improves the appearance, but also helps with broken or brittle feet.

Finally, go all over the horse with a dampened *stable rubber* folded into a flat

bundle, to remove any last traces of dust. The whole grooming process should not take less than half an hour. If it is rushed, the horse will not benefit properly in looks or condition.

The purpose and method of clipping
The heavy winter coat can, however, be a disadvantage to a horse that is expected to work, because it will make him sweat too much. To prevent this, the coat can be clipped. This will not only help to conserve condition, by avoiding heavy sweating, but will also allow the horse to carry out fast work without undue distress. He will be able to work longer, faster and better, and dry off quicker. A clipped coat saves time when grooming, helps to prevent disease, and makes it easier to detect a cut or swelling.

Above: The tail should always be dealt with a few strands of hair at a time. The hair can be separated by holding the tail fairly firmly and shaking a lock or two free. Some grooms prefer to do a tail with their fingers; if this method is used properly the result can be very smart. The use of a body brush is allowed, but not a dandy brush.

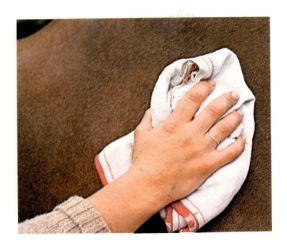

Below: The rubber is normally used to remove any trace of dust after grooming. It should be dampened and made into a flat bundle before being wiped over the coat in the direction of the hair.

Below: A horse's feet should be clean inside and out before the finishing touches are put to the hooves with hoof oil. The oil can be applied from a can with a soft brush, or it may be in a special container with its own brush.

All horses and ponies expected to work during the winter should be clipped. If they are turned out, either a small trace clip or a full trace clip should be sufficient. The animal must have a waterproof New Zealand rug, which should be checked twice a day to make sure that it is not causing chafing.

Trace clipping used to be particularly popular for harness horses: the hair on the under surfaces of the throat and body is removed, and that on the legs and top of the body left long.

For *blanket clipping*, a little more of the hair is removed. This clip is particularly suitable for stabled horses that are being used only for hacking and relatively light work. In this clip, the area normally covered by a blanket is left long, and so is the hair on the legs. The hair on the belly, neck and head is taken off.

A stabled hunter is usually given a *hunter clip*; that is, clipped all over, with the exception of his legs and the saddle patch. The hair on the legs is left long as protection against minor injuries and ailments such as cracked heels and mud fever. The area under the saddle is left in order to absorb sweat and alleviate pressure and chafing.

At the start of the hunting season, some people prefer a full clip for their horses, removing all the coat. For his second clip, the horse gets a normal hunter clip, which provides a little more protection when the weather gets bad. This method has the advantage of making the legs of a rather common animal look rather less hairy than would otherwise be the case.

When the saddle patch is left, care must be taken to ensure that the clip is neat. A useful tip is to clip round an old saddle or numnah. If the saddle patch is too far forward, the horse will look short in the shoulder and long in the back. If, however, the hair is cut straight behind the shoulder and allowed to come well back behind the saddle, the appearance of the animal will often be greatly enhanced – a point to

The hunter clip (left) and the blanket clip (right) are among the most common types of clip for a horse; which clip is selected will depend on the work he has to do, and on whether he is stabled in winter or turned out with a New Zealand rug. The positioning of the saddle patch in the hunter clip can be used to enhance a horse's appearance by making him seem longer or shorter in the back. Skill and practice will prevent any unevenness or clipper marks from showing.

remember when showing off or selling a horse. It requires skill and practice to clip a horse really well without showing any unevenness or clipper marks. Electric clippers are now the most popular, because hand clippers can really only be used effectively for tidying up a horse before a show. The old type of hand-driven clippers are not very satisfactory, and need two people to work them.

The summer coat, being fine and short, should never be clipped. The winter coat is usually given its first clip in early autumn; as it will grow quite quickly, it will need further clips at least every three months, or whenever the coat is more than a centimetre long. Care should be taken that the last winter clip takes place before the summer coat has started to come through.

How to use clippers
Make sure that the clippers are well oiled

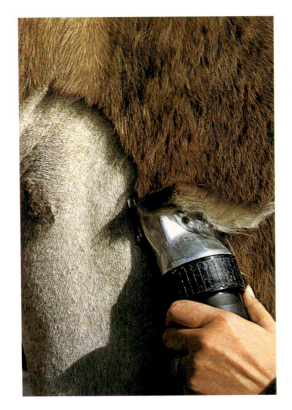

The clippers should be used in the opposite direction from the way the hair grows. Care must be taken to keep them as level as possible and to maintain regular pressure. The mane and tail should be tied out of the way while one is clipping.

and that the blades are sharp. Use the clippers in the opposite direction to the way the hair grows, and keep as level a pressure as possible.

Blunt blades will pull the hair and will also make the clippers overheat: both things that upset a horse. The coat has to be dry before it can be clipped properly, and should preferably be free from grease or grit, which will cause excessive wear on the clipper blades and motor.

The person clipping the horse should wear rubber boots, and should protect long hair with a headscarf. The animal's mane should be tied in bunches, and the tail tied out of the way in an old stocking. Some animals seem to have a natural distrust of being clipped, probably because someone has previously done the job badly. Firm but gentle handling can often allay their fears; but if they refuse to settle, a twitch may have to be used when doing the head. Far better to use a

twitch quickly and get it over with than upset a horse. As a last resort with a really bad case, it may be necessary to ask a veterinary surgeon to give a sedative.

Heels can be trimmed barber-fashion by using a comb and curved scissors. The hair on the back of the heels should not be cut too short, or the skin will become chapped and the horse may get cracked heels.

Some cautionary advice

A horse that has just been clipped will probably feel the cold on first leaving the stable for exercise, and be more inclined to buck and play the fool.

A further word of caution: never clip out a horse's ears. Clipped ears may look smart, but the hair is there to keep out flies and insects, and if a horse gets a fly in his ear he is likely to be very irritated. The correct way is to take a pair of scissors and trim the hair on the ears flush.

8: Horse clothing

The night rug or stable rug can be used with a blanket in winter, not only in the stable, but also when a horse is travelling. The blanket should go over the back longways under the rug, and then be pulled back slightly to make sure that the hair is not ruffled, which would make the horse uncomfortable. The blanket can be folded into a point at the front and then, after the rug has been put on, can be folded neatly over the withers and held in place with a roller. Good-quality blankets, like rugs, are always a sound investment.

Stabled horses, because they cannot exercise themselves enough, need rugs to keep warm. In the summer, they also need protection from flies. When they are travelling, horses require protective clothing and bandages against injury, and when they take part in competitions, they need various other forms of protection to prevent cuts, knocks and strains.

The most common form of stable clothing is the *night rug* or *stable rug*, which is usually made from jute and lined with blanketing. In the winter, a *stable rug* can be used with a blanket. A heavy type of blanket is best, because two or three light ones take longer to put on. And they are more likely to become loose and get trodden on when a horse lies down. The blanket should be placed on the horse's back longways, from ear to tail, and drawn back slightly to smooth the hairs. It should hang down evenly on both sides. The front of the blanket can then be folded back on each side until it comes to a point over the horse's ears. After the stable rug has been put in place, the front of the blanket should then be folded back over the withers, on top of the rug, and held in place with a roller.

Most rollers are about a hand's width wide. The cheaper ones are made from hemp web, wool web or jute web, and the more expensive rollers are made of leather.

In place of the usual jute rug, there are now a number of quite good proprietary brands on sale which are made of other materials. Some rugs have their own surcingles in addition to a breast strap; but I much prefer to use a rug with a separate roller, which can have additional padding to protect the vulnerable part of a horse's spine in the area behind the withers. Rollers should always be fitted very carefully and be very well padded. If the padding is not sufficient, a piece of foam rubber may be used.

Always buy rugs of good quality. They will prove to be less expensive in the long

Left: The only type of rug suitable for use in a field is the New Zealand, made from waterproof materials. There are several varieties.

Right: Summer sheets are made from either cotton or linen, and are used with a surcingle or roller.

run, because they will last longer and stand up to washing much better. Night rugs always become dirty and stained, and need to be cleaned; the cheaper rugs are more inclined to rot and tear.

Make sure, whichever form of rug you use, that it fits loosely round the animal's neck, so that he can lower his head easily to eat. It should not, however, be so loose that it will keep on slipping backwards and chafe his withers. Rugs can be purchased in various sizes; and as well as periodic washing or dry cleaning they should be carefully looked after. When

not in use, they should be stored in a suitably dry cupboard or chest. As they are particularly vulnerable to moths, a few moth balls will be needed as a safeguard.

Using a rug at night

The amount of clothing a horse will need at night should be gauged by the lowest point of temperature reached before morning. A warm evening can quickly turn into a cold night, and it is always safer to rug a horse up well: the top of the stable door can be left open so that he can get plenty

Right: Woollen day rugs are the same shape as stable rugs, and can be bought in a variety of bright colours and bindings.

Left: The Aerborn or sweat sheet is made of a large cotton mesh. It has the same qualities as a string vest.

of fresh air as if he was outside.

A horse's ears should always be warm right to their tips. If they are cold, then an extra blanket will be needed, and the ears should be massaged by gentle pulling until they are warm. When a horse is too hot, he will sweat behind the ears.

Day rugs

Many owners use night rugs during the day but leave off one of the night blankets. *Day rugs* are not essential, but they do look smart, particularly when a horse is travelling to a competition. They are made of a thick, coloured woollen fabric bound with contrasting braid, and usually have the owner's initials sewn in one corner. Like the night rug, they are held in place by a matching surcingle or roller. They also have eyelets at the rear to allow for a braided tail string that helps to prevent the rug from sliding forward.

Sweat rugs and summer sheets

If a horse is wet, either from rain or exercise, the night rug can be put on inside out over an *anti-sweat rug* or a few handfuls of loose straw, and held in place with a roller. The front of the rug can be folded back on each side. A roller must be used because, as the front buckles will be inside out, the rug would otherwise flap about and become dislodged.

The anti-sweat rug is not only of help in the stable when a horse is still sweating, but is also very useful when travelling. It can be placed on a horse when he is hot, either at a show or after hunting, while he is walked around to cool down. Anti-sweat rugs are made of large cotton mesh, and work on the same principle as a string vest. By creating air pockets next to the horse's body, they become a form of insulation which prevents him from becoming chilled. These rugs usually need to be used with a *top sheet*, otherwise the insulating air pockets will not be formed and they cannot work properly. They have to be kept in place with a roller because they tear very easily, particularly if they become dislodged when a horse is rather fresh or gets down to roll.

Summer sheets, which are made of cotton or linen, are usually held in place with a surcingle; they help to keep flies and dust away from a horse in the stable or when travelling. They have a 'fillet string' at the rear attached to loops at each corner; it passes above the hocks and under the tail to prevent a sheet being blown about.

New Zealand rugs
The most useful form of rug for horses turned out during wet or wintry weather is the *New Zealand*. It is usually made of stout canvas and lined with blanketing. Being waterproof, it provides good protection from wind and weather, and enables a trace-clipped horse or pony to winter out quite happily.

The New Zealand rug is the same shape as a normal rug, with one or two straps at the front secured by buckles. But it has additional straps at the back; these cross over each other and pass round the horse's hind legs to hold the rug in position, and stop it from being dislodged when the animal rolls. Many New Zealand rugs also have a surcingle.

When the rug is put on the horse, the front straps should be buckled first and the waterproof pulled gently back so that the hair does not become ruffled underneath. The leg straps are then crossed over and fastened with quick-release clips. On taking the New Zealand rug off, the leg straps must always be undone first, otherwise they can become tangled round the horse's legs when the front of the rug is undone. The correct way of testing that the leg straps, which are adjustable, are the right length is to put a clenched fist between the top of the hind legs and the point where the straps cross over and link.

Some New Zealand rugs also have a neck hood. This may be fitted in particularly bad weather.

Because they get hard wear, through bad weather and through being brushed against branches and hedgerows, New Zealand rugs require constant attention. Cuts and tears must be stitched immediately to prevent rain getting through to the warm blanketing. And the leather straps, which get very wet when a horse lies down in bad weather, need regular greasing to prevent them from getting too hard. The buckles and fastening hooks must also be oiled.

Horses do not really need any other protective clothing when they are stabled, except for bandages, which can be put on a cold horse to get him warm, or they can be used to keep a poultice or leg dressing in place.

There are, however, many items of clothing that are important for protecting a horse when he is travelling or being ridden or driven.

Protecting the tail
A horse in transit will also require a thin and flexible tail bandage. This will prevent the top part of the tail from being rubbed

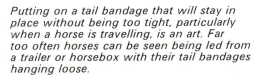

Putting on a tail bandage that will stay in place without being too tight, particularly when a horse is travelling, is an art. Far too often horses can be seen being led from a trailer or horsebox with their tail bandages hanging loose.

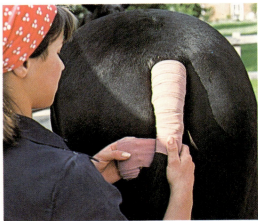

Left: To apply a tail bandage, first damp the hair then place one hand under the tail and unroll about 8 inches (20 cm) of bandage.

Hold the rolled-up bandage in the other hand, and put the loose end under the tail, holding it firmly. Keep hold of the tail until the loose end is secured by the bandage being wound evenly down the tail. Then wind the bandage back up the tail and fasten it neatly with the tapes, using a double bow.

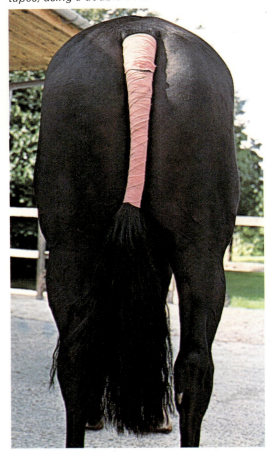

Right: The tail can then be bent back into a comfortable position. To take the bandage off, grasp it nearest the dock and slide it downwards with both hands.

and damaged when he leans against the side of the box or partition to keep his balance. A tail bandage should not be too tight, particularly if it is put on when the tail or the bandage is damp. A tail guard may also be used. A guard is made of soft leather or thick woollen cloth; it is secured in place by tapes and an adjustable leather strap that runs from the top of the guard to the roller.

Protecting the head

A head guard, usually made of padded leather with ear holes, or a single strip of foam rubber, is often put over a horse's poll to prevent him banging his head when travelling. This is particularly important when a trailer is being used.

Protecting the legs

Two different types of bandages are essential. Stable bandages, which protect a horse when he is being transported, are made of woollen fabric or flannel about 8 cm (3 in) wide and 2.25 metres (7 or 8 ft) in length. Two tapes are sewn at one end to hold the bandages in place on the horse's leg. Some owners save money by making their own stable bandages out of lengths of blanketing.

To put a bandage on, it should first be neatly rolled, with the tapes folded in the middle, and then applied to the leg beginning just below the knee or hock. The bandage is wound downwards round the leg and fetlock joint as far as the coronet band, and is then wound upwards again. The tapes can be tied neatly below the knee; the knot should be on the outside of the cannon bone, never on the tendons. Stable bandages must not be put on tightly. They should be just firm enough to prevent them from slipping down. A layer of gamgee tissue or foam rubber may be put under a bandage to give additional warmth and protection during a journey.

Exercise and working bandages, which give a degree of stretch, must always be put on over cotton wool or better still gamgee tissues. They should be sewn in place for cross-country riding; but some competitors put strips of sticky tape over the bows holding the bandages in place, and this is a quicker and more effective method of ensuring that they do not come undone.

On the front legs, working bandages are positioned between the knee and the fetlock joint. On the hind legs, they come from just below the hock to the fetlock.

Knee caps and hock boots are also valuable items of clothing for protecting vulnerable areas. The knee cap consists of a strong stiff leather pad, usually set in fabric. At the top, there is a well-padded leather strap, which buckles fairly tightly above the knee and prevents the knee cap from slipping. The lower strap is buckled loosely below the knee in such a way that the joint can bend normally: its function is to prevent the knee cap turning upwards.

Knee caps are often used when a horse is being ridden on the road to prevent injury to the knees if for any reason he slips or is brought down. Some riders do not consider that they give much protection, but they are certainly better than nothing.

The hock boot is rather similar to the knee cap and is fixed top and bottom by leather straps. Its main purpose is to prevent injuries to the hocks if the horse backs up hard against the box.

The purpose of boots

Various types of boots are used to save a horse from knocks and cuts. The lighter type of five strap felt or leather brushing boot gives good protection against occasional brushing – that is, when a horse hits one foreleg or hindleg with the other as he moves. Another effective and simple device is the rubber ring.

While a horse is galloping or is landing over a jump, a fetlock can come into contact with the ground; when that happens a boot covering the heel will save damage

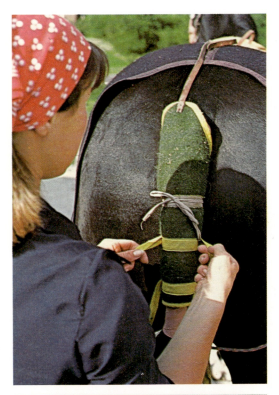

from flints and stones. Over-reaches (touching the front leg with the hind leg) when jumping also often occur low down on the heel, and the best protection is an over-reach boot. It should be made of fairly thin rubber so that it is elastic enough to pull easily over the hoof, but it must be small enough to fit snugly on the foot without going up the leg.

A more damaging type of injury can occur from a horse striking into itself around the joint and at the back of the tendon. To reduce this risk, tendon boots should be worn. They are shaped to the leg, and have a strong leather-covered pad at the rear.

There are also shin boots, sometimes worn by show jumpers, to protect the front of their horse's legs.

Left: A tail guard made from soft leather, canvas or rugging is a very useful item of clothing when travelling. It goes on over a tail bandage, and completely covers the dock area of the tail.

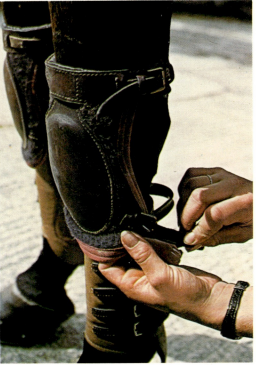

Left: Knee-caps are also used during travelling or walking exercise as protection against a horse slipping and hurting himself. They should be tied fairly tightly at the top, with the lower strap loose. Most knee-caps are made from felt, reinforced with blocked leather at the knees. Other forms of knee-cap are used for jumping and polo.

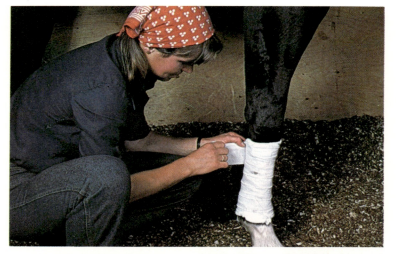

Exercising bandages, sometimes called pressure or support bandages, can be used to give protection against thorns and brambles, though their main purpose is to support the back tendons and to reinforce tendons that are weak or strained.
They must always be put on with a degree of firmness from below the knee to just above the fetlock joint.

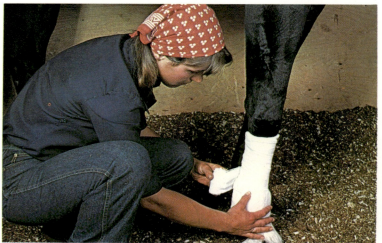

Start by unrolling about 10 inches (25 cm) of bandage, and hold it at an angle across the leg, close to the knee. Wind one turn round the leg, and allow the spare end to fall down the leg. Then wind the rest of the bandage over the spare end down the leg. When the fetlock joint is reached, turn up the remaining part of the spare end and wind the bandage back up the leg towards the starting point. The bandage can then be secured with its own tapes, or can be taped down for greater security.

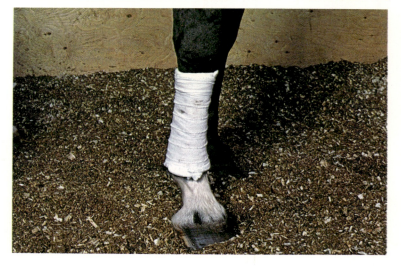

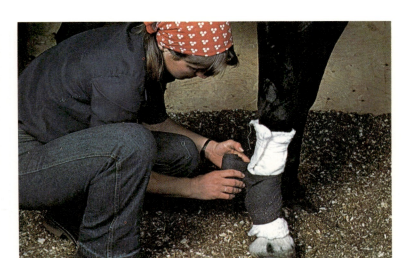

Stable bandages made of wool provide warmth, comfort and protection. They are applied to cover as much of the leg as possible from the knee or hock down to the coronet. To put on a bandage, it should first be rolled, with the tapes neatly folded across the width of the material, and the sewn side inwards. It can be used with cotton wool or gamgee.

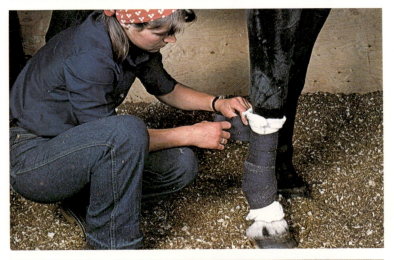

Start bandaging just below the knee or hock, and wind the bandage round the leg until the coronet is reached. Then take the bandage back up the leg, as evenly as possible, until the material is used up. But do not go any higher than the starting point.

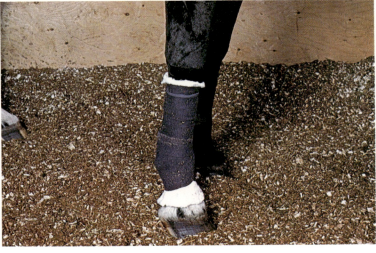

The tapes should then be tied so that the bow or other knot lies either to the outside or the inside of the leg. It must never lie to the rear, where it can press on the tendons, or to the front, where it can press on the bone.

9: Stable routine and hygiene

The routine of a stable often has to be a sensible compromise between the welfare of the horse and the needs and daily commitments of his owner. Years ago, people would not have thought of keeping a horse for pleasure unless they could afford to employ a groom. Few owners now are lucky enough to have help in their stables, and most have to arrange their time so that they can look after their horse, and also, perhaps, run a house, or tackle a full-time job.

Some form of established routine must be worked out and adhered to, or the horse's welfare will suffer and so will his ability to give pleasure. If shortage of time is not a major problem, and if you are good at getting up early in the morning, the following timetable may be suitable. It can be varied to suit individual needs.

Trotting up hill is an excellent way of putting on muscle, but care should be taken not to affect the movement of the shoulders of a dressage horse. This sort of exercise must only take place after the steady walking and trotting stages have been completed and the horse is fit.

7.30 am Check and refill the water buckets, skip out the stable if shavings are being used, or muck out if the horse is on straw, leaving a thin cover-

A rider should always walk the first mile out and the last mile home. A tired horse will always appreciate the rider taking the weight off his back, and many riders will dismount to walk the last ten minutes or so.

ing over the floor and the remainder stacked against the walls.

Feed and let the horse have a section of hay.

8.45 am Give the horse a quick brush over and remove any stable marks or stains.

9.15 am Tack up and set out for exercise.

10.45 am Return from exercise and unsaddle. If a schooling session is to take place during the exercise period, this should not usually last for more than 20–30 minutes. The horse will appreciate a gentle hack afterwards.

10.50 am Groom thoroughly.

11.30 am Give the horse a good feed of hay and leave him to enjoy it without interference.

12 noon Clean tack thoroughly, including headcollar.

12.45 pm Replenish water buckets, pick up droppings, and put down bedding if straw is being used.

1.15 pm Lunch-time feed and hay.

5.30 pm Fill water buckets. Straighten all rugs, pick up droppings, add fresh shavings or straw, and bed down ready for the night.

6.00 pm Give last feed of the day and remainder of hay ration.

9.00 pm Last look round. Fill up water buckets and ensure rugs are straight and horse is contented and comfortable.

Going out to work

On hunting or competition days, the routine would have to be changed to take into account the time of the meet or the start of the competition. Never, however, feed hay in the morning if a horse has to gallop and jump before noon, and only give a small feed of concentrates if the

73

horse has to work within two hours of it.

Before leaving the stable on a hunting morning, make arrangements for a warm linseed or bran mash to be ready on the horse's return. During the course of the day, save his legs as much as possible; and whenever a suitable opportunity occurs, dismount. This will not only relieve the horse of your weight for a few minutes, but also give him an opportunity to stale more easily.

When you have had a good run, be satisfied. The majority of horses love hunting and will continue to appear keen and full of running after they are, in fact, tired. It is then that strains can occur.

If the horse is being boxed home, get off and slacken the girth on the way to the box. Walk him for about 20 minutes to allow him to cool before removing his saddle, rugging him up and bandaging him in readiness for the journey. He can then have a short drink of water.

If you are hacking home, cover as much of the journey as you can at a steady jog. Remember that it is easier for a tired horse to trot along the road than on a grass verge that will probably be rutted and uneven. A mile from home, dismount, slacken the girth, and lead him the rest of the way. This will help any saddle stiffness you may have, as well as help to cool the horse.

Back in the stable

When you reach the stable, give your horse a drink of chilled water and some hay to nibble. Provided that the evening is not too cold or dark, leave his rugs off for a few minutes. If you have a small paddock near the stable, let him have a good roll, which will freshen him up and get rid of any stiffness. If not, let him loose in the box without rugs for a short while so that he has time to stale and roll if he wants to. Then put a handful of clean straw on his back, with a blanket and rug on top without a roller. This will allow the air to circulate and dry any wet areas,

Right: Long and patient training can culminate in competition success for the ambitious rider with the right horse, or just in hours of pleasure for those whose horses may not quite have the ability to get into the ribbons at top class events. Thousands of riders rarely win a prize but are quite happy joining in the fun of competing, and knowing that they are getting the best out of the horses they have worked with and trained.

Right: When a competition or a day's hunting is over, the welfare and comfort of the horse must come first. A rider must always make sure that his horse is cool and has stopped blowing before being given a drink or anything to eat, even a lump of sugar. The horse can be walked round in a sweat sheet covered by his stable rug or travelling rug put on inside-out. Then he can enjoy a few nibbles of hay while his travelling bandages are applied in readiness for the journey home.

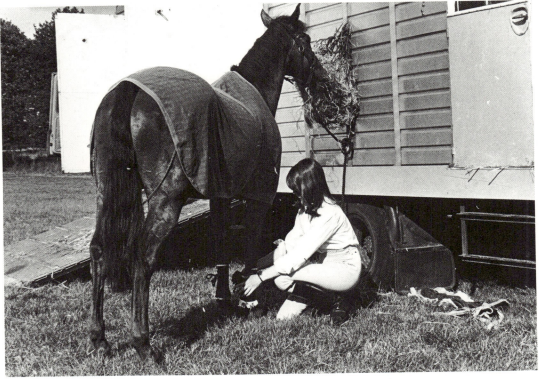

particularly in the region of the saddle patch.

If the horse's legs are wet and muddy, some old woollen stable bandages will help to dry them off and keep him warm. Tie him up so that he cannot get down to roll, and give him his mash and some more hay.

As the horse will be tired, the end of the day's grooming should be kept to a minimum. Any dried mud must be removed, of course, and his legs and quarters examined for thorns, scratches and cuts. Minor injuries can be treated with either tincture of iodine or one of the proprietary disinfectant powder sprays. A clean set of wool bandages will help to keep him warm, and also perhaps prevent any tendency his legs may have to fill or swell.

The horse can then be rugged up for the night. If he sweats up again – and you can easily tell by feeling under his rugs – he will have to be walked round with a sweat sheet or dried off with a wisp. He may otherwise catch a chill. His ears should be warm and dry and you must pull them gently if they are cold. When you are sure that he is all right, his water buckets can be replenished and he can be given his normal evening meal and a good feed of hay. Then look in on him last thing at night to see that he is all right and not suffering from overtiredness.

The following morning, run him up in hand to make sure that he is sound. If he is, an hour's gentle walking exercise is all that should be necessary.

Stable hygiene

Whatever you use your horse for, your main aim should be to keep him in good health, so that he develops as few ailments as possible. Cleanliness and hygiene are very important. However good the drainage system is in a stable or stable yard, some strong disinfectant must be poured into the drains at regular intervals. If mangers are being used, make sure that they are kept really clean. A horse's

sense of smell is very much more acute than that of a human being, and old, sour food will in time put him off eating and will also attract vermin.

The stable walls must be kept clean. Some people still maintain that cobwebs in the roof of the stable are healthy and catch dust and flies, but I cannot believe that they are correct.

I always like to see dogs and cats about a stable yard, provided that the dogs are well trained. Accustoming horses to the company of dogs makes them less likely to be disturbed by any dogs they meet on a ride, or by hounds when they are taken hunting. A good stable cat will keep down the rats and mice, and horses usually enjoy their company.

A well-trained dog around the stable yard is not only a pleasant sight, but, more important, it helps the horses to get used to other animals. A hunter will be far less likely to kick out at a hound if he is used to the family dog. And when a horse is out at exercise and meets a stray dog who yaps at his heels, he will be less inclined to use the situation as an excuse to misbehave.

10: The importance of good shoeing

A good, experienced farrier is an essential member of the team needed to keep horses fit and well, and to cure their ills when they get into trouble. Unfortunately, few shoeing forges are left, but there are travelling farriers who will visit horses on a regular basis. A horse in work needs to have his shoes removed about every three or four weeks, even if they are not worn enough to be replaced by new ones. Otherwise the shoes can pinch because of the growth of the hoof.

Horses were never intended to carry the weight of a rider or perform many of the tasks that now seem to have become second nature to them. The foot of an average horse has an area of only a few square centimetres, and yet it has to support half a ton of horse and rider, and absorb the strain and concussions of galloping and jumping.

When jumping, the weight and strain is often taken on one fore foot. It is not surprising that the phrase 'no foot, no horse' is one of the most quoted sayings in the horse world.

The horse is not naturally prone to lameness. It is only when he is expected to carry a rider's weight over a variety of different surfaces for long periods, and at speeds greater than those at which a horse would normally travel, that difficulties sometimes arise.

The purpose of shoeing
It is to try to prevent soreness, and stop a horse's feet from breaking, that metal shoes are nailed to the walls of the hooves. The shoes are bound to have some effect on the natural functioning of the hooves,

Often, when a horse jumps a fence, all the weight, including that of the rider, has to be taken on one foot. Consequently, he needs not only to be shod properly, but also to have as much protection as possible. This protection may be in the form of bandages, supporting the tendons, or of boots which are specially designed to also protect the legs and underneath the heel.

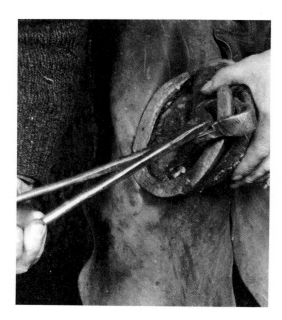

Above: With either hot or cold shoeing, the farrier first removes the old shoe by cutting off all the clenches with his buffer and driving hammer, and levering the shoe off with his pincers. If the clenches have been cut cleanly, the wall of the hoof should not be broken or torn. The farrier then uses a drawing knife to trim the ragged parts of the sole and frog before rasping a level bearing surface.

but how great an effect depends very much on the skill of the farrier and the way in which the horse is shod.

A number of bones are encased within the hoof. There are layers of sensitive flesh around them, known as *laminae*. Although the walls and sole are rigid, the inner part of the foot is capable of limited movement because of the rubber-like quality of the frog. The frog is the triangular wedge at the back of the sole, where the wall of the foot ends on either side of the heel.

The frog takes much of the horse's weight, and absorbs the concussion when the foot comes in contact with the ground. As it does so, it becomes depressed, expands, and forces the ends of the wall slightly outwards, enabling the inner structure to move.

When a hoof is damaged, its stiff box-like frame causes problems because it cannot swell in the way that other parts of the body do when subjected to severe concussion or abnormal strain. This inability to swell can give rise to serious complications that, in some instances, can aggravate the condition to such an extent that the bones become deformed or pushed out of place. The horse can be made permanently unsound.

When an injury can be reached, it can usually be treated and any inflammation reduced. But when there is an injury within the hoof, treatment is obviously very much more difficult. That is why many types of foot lameness in horses tend to be permanent. And some form of inflammation is present in all injuries and other diseases of the feet.

Because of the serious nature of foot problems in horses and ponies, those looking after them should know something of the structure and working of a hoof. And they must ensure that every animal is shod frequently. A horse doing heavy work may have to be shod every three weeks or so.

The wall of a healthy hoof grows con-

tinuously at the rate of more than 1 cm (about half an inch) a month. Because nattural growth is impossible when shoes are nailed to the wall, they have to be removed, and the wall trimmed at frequent intervals. Otherwise the foot will become misshapen. Additional strain will also be placed on the fetlocks, tendons and suspensory ligaments.

The work of the farrier

A good blacksmith or farrier will examine a shoe before he removes it to see whether any part has had undue wear. He will then know whether anything should be done to correct a possible fault in a horse's action. If he has any doubt, he may ask to see a horse run up, and suggest either building up or lowering the sides of the shoe to get the horse's weight distributed more evenly.

Before replacing the shoe, he will cut down the wall of the hoof and rasp it level, being careful not to damage the frog or the sole of the foot. As the frog is the leg's natural shock absorber, it must be able to come in contact with the ground when the new shoe is in place.

A shoe should always be made to fit the foot. The foot should never be rasped to fit the shoe. Cold shoeing, when the shoe is not heated, can never be as satisfactory as the old hot shoeing method; but provided that the blacksmith knows the horse and makes up his shoes specially, there are unlikely to be problems.

With hot shoeing, each shoe is heated until it is red hot. By holding it onto the hoof, the blacksmith can see whether it fits properly. If it does, it will leave a brown burn mark all the way round the wall.

After the new shoe has been made and fitted (top), it is nailed in place (left). The first nail to be driven in is usually one at the toe. The end of the nail, where it penetrates the wall, is turned over and twisted off, forming a clench. This is tidied up with a rasp and hammered flat.

When the shoe is cooled and nailed onto the hoof, the clenches (nail ends) should be evenly spaced in a line around the foot. The ends are then turned over and hammered down, before being rasped to remove the rough edges. The surface of the wall of the foot, which prevents the horn absorbing water, should not be damaged in this process. If the nails are not driven in correctly, they will pinch the foot, or prick the laminae, causing blood poisoning or the formation of an abscess. This is more difficult to prevent when the wall of the foot is particularly thin, leaving little room for the nails.

Shoes are rather more than plain semi-circles of iron. They usually have clips to hold them in position and each shoe has a groove, known as a 'fuller', running round the side that comes into contact with the ground, to give a better grip. Calkins can also help improve the foot-hold. They are made by turning over the metal at the heel to form a sort of small step.

Studs and pads

The farrier will provide screw holes in the shoe to allow studs of various shapes and sizes to be screwed in before a horse goes jumping or travels along a slippery road. When not required, the studs can be removed with a plain spanner and the hole filled with a plug of oily cotton wool. If the thread becomes damaged, the hole can be cleaned and sometimes repaired with a

Studs made of special metal can be fitted into the heels of shoes to give additional grip. They can be screwed into the shoe with an ordinary spanner in a matter of minutes. The studs vary in shape according to whether a horse is going to travel along a slippery road, in which case he would require small pointed studs, or is going jumping, when the studs would be larger for the soft ground.

metal 'tap' the same size as the metal thread on the stud.

Leather pads are also sometimes placed by the blacksmith over the foot and held in place by the shoe. They protect the sole of the foot from sharp flints and stones. These pads are particularly valuable when a horse has to be exercised in stony country, or has to gallop across soft flinty ground when hunting or in cross-country events. The pads also help to absorb any additional shock to the feet when the ground is especially hard. They must, however, be removed at regular intervals.

11: Exercising

A young horse can often start his jumping
career by being schooled over low cavaletti.
These are movable wooden jumps usually
made of poles about 9 feet (2·75 metres)
long that rest at either end on stout cross-
poles. In Germany they are better known as
Bodenricks. Schooling fences for a young
horse should not be high, and should be
always well within his scope and judgement.

Horses, particularly those kept on their own, can suffer badly from boredom and loneliness. They look forward to their daily exercise because it provides a change of scenery and gives them an opportunity to see other horses and people.

Exercising, however, must not be confused with schooling. The daily exercise should be fun for horse and rider, a time when both can relax and enjoy the countryside. The route should be varied each day as much as possible, so that there is something fresh to look at and different situations to be met. But schooling is a time for concentration and discipline, a time for instruction.

The advice given in *Peri Hippikes*, the first known work on the training of the riding horse, written by Xenophon, the Greek historian, philosopher and cavalryman, is as true today as it no doubt was when the book was written more than 2,000 years ago.

Xenophon wrote: 'The gods have given to men the power of instructing each other in their duties by word of mouth, which is denied to a horse . . . But if you can reward him when he obeys as you wish and punish him when he is disobedient, he will then learn to know his duty. This rule can be said to apply to the whole art of horsemanship.'

A horse needs a combination of exercise and schooling if he is to be happy and is to give real pleasure to his rider. Unless a horse is trained, he will find many of the movements he is asked to perform beyond his capabilities, whether in dressage or in jumping. The result will be that he will become muddled, and the more muddled he gets, the more bad tempered, nervous and nappy he will become.

The problems and purpose of schooling

The rider must, of course, have reached a stage of training that enables him to convey his wishes distinctly, without confusing the horse. A rider who has never experienced the feel of a well-trained animal will not really know what he is trying to achieve.

Schooling, then, should be left to horsemen who have the necessary knowledge and experience to teach; and, even more important, to know exactly what it is they are trying to convey. Unless the teacher can gain the horse's confidence, trust and respect, he will never end up with a quiet, happy and obedient animal anxious to please.

So often one hears inexperienced riders saying that they have bought a young horse to 'school on', despite the fact that they have not developed the necessary understanding or skill to make a success of the task. The sad result is usually a soured, ill-tempered horse, with a bad mouth and manners, doomed to a life of misery. The rider is frustrated and cannot understand why other people's horses always seem so much more fun than his own. Very many horses are ruined by riders who neither know what they are trying to achieve nor how to achieve it.

When schooling a horse, do not try and teach more than you know. If you reach a stage when you are getting out of your depth, seek good professional advice. It will save you time and money in the long run, and you will have a much more satisfactory horse to ride and enjoy. Never be afraid to admit you do not know. That is the sign of a novice. Experienced riders are always prepared to learn, and some top riders still have trainers to whom they turn for advice when they have a problem with their horse or their riding.

A person schooling a horse should try to achieve confidence, happiness and obedience. Every effort should be made to prevent the horse becoming frightened or unduly excited, and the training should never be rushed. Progress should be gradual, so that the animal hardly realizes that he is being asked to do anything really new.

Perseverance and almost limitless

When a horse has done well, he will always appreciate a word of encouragement and, possibly, a titbit. Even a mouthful of sweet grass is enough to tell him that his rider is pleased with him. Firm treatment is an important factor in every horse's training, but so is kindness and understanding. Most horses like to please their riders, provided that they are encouraged to do so. They are more intelligent than many people are prepared to give them credit for; and once they understand what is required, they will often tackle a task with enthusiasm, particularly when they know that there is probably a treat at the end. If a horse is naughty and needs to be admonished with more than the rider's voice, he should be given a sharp whack behind the girth with a stick immediately he does something wrong. Then the incident should be forgotten.

patience are essential qualities. Experience, nerve and brilliant horsemanship will not succeed if a rider is not temperamentally suited to the task of schooling, and it would be much better to leave it to somebody else.

The horse and schooling

A horse's actions and behaviour are prompted by the mixture of instinct and intelligence needed for his survival in the wild. The basic aim of schooling or training should be to graft a habit of obedience onto his natural instincts. This is possible because a horse is not only a creature of habit but also one with a good retentive memory. If treated properly, he is prepared to trust people and accept their domination without resentment.

Even wild horses in herds are used to being dominated by a 'boss horse' or leader. Once this domination has been established, a horse will usually settle down quietly, provided that he gets enough food and is not unfairly treated. If he becomes upset, his actions will usually be spontaneous and prompted by instinct.

A horse reacts to people in much the same way as he reacts to other horses. At first, he is cautious and ready to defend himself. But once he decides that you are not a threat to his existence, he will probably try and dominate you and become 'boss'. If you show signs of fear, he will get bolder and eventually you will have a fight on your hands. If, however, you stand your ground, he will soon sense that he has been unable to intimidate you, and you will have gone a long way towards achieving his respect.

Horses will challenge authority from time to time. But they will usually give warning of their intentions if they intend to develop an ordinary disobedience into a battle.

Never force a show-down if you can help it. You will be no match for a horse's strength. Tact and guile are more likely

Above: When a horse is fit he will enjoy a really good 'pipe opener' to clear his wind and lungs. A really fit horse will need plenty of room to gallop safely and to pull up as here, and the choice of ground is important in order to minimize the risk of damage to tendons, or perhaps a bruised sole. And, of course, on public land a horse should never be ridden in a way that will cause inconvenience or danger to others.

Left: This horse is collected and nicely under control. A great deal of patient schooling has no doubt been necessary before the horse would perform in this way, but the results are well worth while.

to win the day than brute force. If a horse once realizes that he can use his strength to become 'boss', he will become a problem horse and your task will be made very much more difficult.

If punishment is necessary, it should be short and sharp and administered at the time of the offence, so that the horse is fully aware of why he is being punished. Once he has learnt his lesson, let him know that you are pleased with him. Then find something more interesting and enjoyable for him to do.

To strike a horse in the stable is an unforgivable sin. If you do, he will start to despise you and will turn sour. All horses are extremely sensitive, and the better bred they are the more acute this sensitivity becomes. They see situations and actions as either pleasant or unpleasant. They need to be understood; a thoughtless act, probably carried out in the heat of the moment, may undo months of careful training, and ruin the trust and understanding built up between horse and rider.

Curing bad habits

Most horses like to please. A display of exuberance may only be caused by a horse's desire to show you what he can do. If he is treated too harshly, he will not understand and may become sour. A rider should never try to treat a bad habit, but rather try to find out the cause of it.

A horse may be nervous and need soothing, or he may be of a sluggish, lazy nature and need encouragement. If he snorts or flinches and lays back his ears, he may be associating what is happening with some previous bad experience or rough treatment. His natural instinct tells him to get away from the situation as quickly as possible, and he will need to be reassured that everything is going to be all right and he has nothing to fear.

In time, all horses will respond to the right treatment, once the rider has established complete confidence and the horse

can understand the reasons for his actions. Horses will respond to orders they have been trained to understand, because in the main they enjoy their work. They are always anxious to please and show how clever they are, even if it means showing off a little. Horses can be very vain, and they know when they have done well. Watch a show jumper coming into the ring to collect his prize and do a lap of honour!

If a horse continues to misbehave or behave out of character, take a moment to reflect whether you are to blame. There may be something wrong that you should have noticed. He may be trying to tell you about a bad tooth or an ill-fitting bit or saddle. No amount of firm handling or punishment will cure that sort of situation. All horses can be aggravating at times; but if you feel you are losing patience with a horse, put him back into the stable or into his field until you have cooled down. If you let him see that you have lost your temper, you will have lost the battle as well as the horse's respect. Remember that, just as with human beings, some horses possess a slower intelligence than others, and will take longer to grasp the significance of the various aids. Horses also vary in their natural ability and courage.

A horse may refuse at a jump or misbehave because he is frightened and cannot understand what is required of him. He may also lack confidence, and not realize that he can tackle the obstacle without being hurt. If he follows another horse, he may realize that there is nothing to fear. Once he understands what is being asked of him, he will then begin to carry out his rider's wishes happily as a matter of course.

Short periods of schooling followed by a hack, when the horse can relax his body and mind, will yield much better results than long sessions. There is a limit to how much a horse's mind can absorb and retain in one session. There is no point in trying to force him to learn too much at a time. He will forget most of it, and the lesson will have to be learnt all over again.

The aims of exercising

When exercising, always be on guard for trouble; but remember that exercise time is also meant to be the horse's fun time. A few exhibitions of high spirits, providing that there is no danger from traffic, should not be dealt with too severely as long as the situation is not allowed to get out of hand. Let your horse have a fairly loose rein when he is walking, so that he can stretch and feel free. Then, when you shorten the reins, he will immediately know that you want to give him some instructions and will be ready for them.

Horses enjoy company, and it is always more pleasant for horse and rider to be able to exercise with others. In the case of young horses, a more experienced animal can be used for giving a lead, or for helping to steady them if they get excited for any reason.

Try to exercise in company with other horses as much as possible. It is more enjoyable for you and the horse, because horses always go better in company and appreciate companionship. A horse nearing home, where he knows he will find food and drink, will often put on pace and stride out very much better. If you decide to go away from home, or leave the company of others, he may show his displeasure and disappointment by a display of temperament. When that happens, let him know that he has to go where you want, at the pace you decide. If you are firm, he will soon get the message.

Rules for exercising

Before you leave the stable, always check that tack is correctly fitted and the horse is comfortable. If your horse is in a stall, turn him round before you tighten up the girth or you will strain the tree of the saddle. Never leave a horse loose in a box with his saddle on, or he may roll and damage it; and it is the most expensive item of saddlery that you have. If a horse is inclined to be cold-backed, put the saddle on about half an hour before you plan to leave, and do not tighten the girth until you are due to start. You can always leave him tied up, with a rug over the saddle.

Do not leave the stable yard at a trot. Let the horse walk for the first ten minutes, and then jog quietly on. Trotting on the road wears out the shoes and puts additional strain on the feet and legs. There are some who say it hardens a horse's legs; they are welcome to their opinion and the vet's bills!

Let your horse walk the last ten minutes; if he is not fit or is feeling tired, dismount and walk beside him. When you reach the stable, leave him loose in his box for a few minutes after the tack has been removed, to give him a chance to relieve himself and have a roll.

Lady Apsley, a fine horsewoman, used to say that the mark of a good horseman

was his ability to act quickly. 'One notices with all good horsemen how quick they are, quick to notice a little thing, quick to get on, quick to get off, quick to think, quick to act.' This observation is still true today.

How much exercise

The amount of exercise a horse needs depends a great deal on how fit he is and the amount of food he is getting. Horses must always be introduced to exercise gradually, because over-exertion can have serious effects when the horse is only partially fit, and can sometimes cause permanent damage.

After a horse has come up from grass, or has had a forced rest through illness, he should be allowed only walking exercise on the road for the first few weeks. His legs will then harden up and will be able to stand the jarring of more strenuous work. As he becomes fitter, the duration

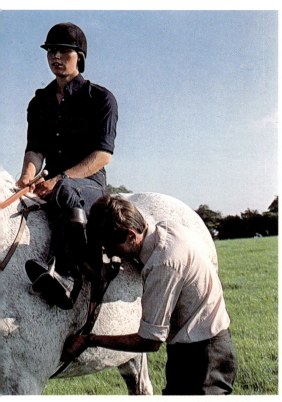

Left: If a horse appears to be fit but still becomes short of breath after steady exercise, his heart and wind should be checked by a veterinary surgeon. If the horse appears to be sound, the veterinary surgeon may suggest carrying out a blood count to see whether it is suffering from anaemia, which may need treatment.

Below: Steady walking exercise is the only way to get a horse fit after he has been turned out for his holidays, or has been out of action because of illness or injury. Some horses are inclined to get excited in company and will not settle down to a steady walk. In such cases, they must be taken out on their own and persuaded to walk instead of getting into a lather. There is no short cut to getting a horse fit and ready for fast work except weeks of walking. This may be boring, but the rider can always use the time to plan the fun they will have together when the horse is fit.

of the exercise can be extended, and he can be given an occasional trot. The rider will be able to sense when the horse is ready for faster work.

After about a month, a short trot and a steady canter can be included in the routine. A stiff gallop every two or three days can be allowed after about six or seven weeks of steady work. Some horses, because of size or temperament, take longer to get fit than others. But the process must never be rushed, and an owner must learn to judge how a horse is progressing. Even when you think your horse is fit, the first competition or full day's hunting will probably catch him out. You will have to let him ease up when he finds the pace too much.

How to achieve peak condition

Top condition cannot be retained indefinitely, or a horse will start to go 'over the top' and become stale. The art of good training is to bring a horse to the peak

of condition at just the right time, and to keep him there as long as possible.

Work on hills is one of the best ways of getting a horse fit. But hillwork is demanding, and should be taken gradually. When the time comes for you to give a horse a gallop uphill, you will soon see how fit he really is.

After the legs have become hard without any signs of puffiness, and the neck and back muscles have begun to develop and harden, schooling can begin. It should start with sessions of only a few minutes each day. In this way, a horse's strength and memory will not be overtaxed, and he will remember the lessons of the previous day.

Every horse should have somewhere to go and have a really good roll, not only when he is turned out to grass but also occasionally after a work period. He will get real pleasure from his freedom to stretch and roll, and only a lazy rider would deny him his treat. A few extra minutes grooming is a small price to pay for a horse's comfort and relaxation after he has carried his rider well.

After the first weeks, the schooling sessions can be cut to every other day, or perhaps to twice a week.

When it is time for your horse to have his holiday, he will need to be 'roughed off' ready to go out into the field. In the spring, this will usually take about two weeks. During that time, his ration of concentrates, such as oats and nuts, will have to be reduced and replaced with bran, hay and carrots and other types of roots. All fast work should be stopped, and his exercise periods restricted to walking and trotting. His blankets can be taken off after a few days, and his rug left off altogether about a week before he is due to be turned out.

A horse given his liberty after being stabled may gallop about and get into trouble. It is wise to exercise him first so that he is fairly tired. Do not give him a morning feed; let him feel hungry. The chances are that when he has had a canter round and explored various parts of the field, he will get his head down to graze, and will start to enjoy his period of rest.

12: Preparing for competitions

When you are sure your horse is fit and has had the necessary schooling, he may be ready for his first competition. You will have to decide whether you want to take part in showing, show jumping or horse trials. The entries will need to be made in good time, and your horse will have to be got ready to do justice to himself and to you.

There is an old saying 'competitions are won at home'; and there is quite a lot of truth in it. It is the responsibility of the trainer or owner to make sure that a horse has been entered for the right class and type of competition, and to see that he arrives at the ground in plenty of time, looking his best, properly shod and in the right frame of mind. The rider has to make sure that the horse knows exactly what is expected of him.

Horses quickly get to know when they are off to a competition. They sense the change in routine, the slight feeling of tension and the additional attention to detail. The moment plaiting starts, they are usually left in no doubt; and they will start to enjoy not only the fussing but also the thought of going somewhere new, and doing something different.

How to make a horse look his best

Whatever the competition, every horse should be made to look well in deference to the judges. A badly turned-out horse is a credit to no one, least of all to his owner. Animals may differ in ability, conformation and experience, but there is no reason why they should not all be made to look their best. It is only a question of knowledge and effort.

Top right: If the horse is to have a bang tail instead of a pointed switch tail, the end should be cut off squarely, level with the points of the hocks. While the cutting is being done, an assistant will be needed to put an arm beneath the root of the tail so that afterwards it will be naturally square.

Left: A well pulled tail considerably improves a horse's appearance. To pull a tail, start at the dock region, removing all the hair from underneath. This should be done a little at a time, either with the fingers or by winding a few hairs round the teeth of a metal comb.

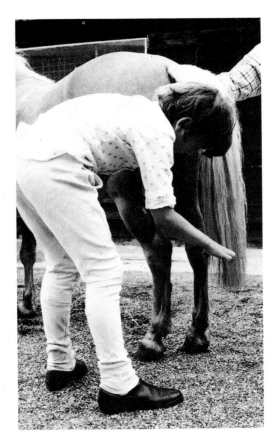

Preparation of the tail

Tails and manes should be pulled. An unruly mane can be hogged (cut short), but this only looks good on a cob-type horse. A tail must never be trimmed with a clipping machine. It will take months to recover, and will end up looking like a brush.

The correct way to pull a tail is, first, to remove all tangles and separate out the hairs. Then, stand opposite the hind quarters and pull the hairs growing underneath, a few at a time, with the aid of a mane comb. The hairs should be removed with a sharp tug, either with the fingers or by winding them round the comb, or you will pull hairs that you do not want to remove. A little resin on the fingers will help.

Only the hairs at the dock end should be removed. The end of the tail can be squared off as a 'bang tail' by getting someone to place an arm beneath the tail's root, while you cut the hair off squarely, level with the points of the hocks. Or the tail should be left as a 'switch tail' by pulling the hairs on either side to about halfway down, and letting the ends grow to a natural point.

After it has been pulled, the tail should be damped slightly and be put in a tail bandage to keep it in shape. The bandage must not be too tight, or it will irritate and cause a nasty sore.

Preparation of the mane

For a mane to be plaited properly, it needs to be thin and silky and about a hand's width in length. If it has a tendency to fall down on both sides of the neck, it will need thinning out underneath. The longest hairs should be dealt with first. They are wound round the finger and removed a few at a time. Never pull the top hairs, or any hairs which may stand up after plaiting, otherwise they will form a sort of upright fringe along the crest. A mane need not be pulled all in one go. The best results are frequently obtained by pulling a little at a time.

If you decide your horse's mane should be 'hogged', remember that doing so will leave him with little protection from the flies in summer. To hog a mane, you should get a friend to place his arm round the top of your horse's head, just behind the poll, and gradually draw it downwards. While his head is lowered, you can run the clippers along each side of the mane from withers to poll. There will then be a ridge along the middle which can easily be removed. As soon as the hairs start to grow again, usually after about ten days, the process will need to be repeated. The part of the mane where the bridle rests should be taken off with the scissors. To persuade an unruly mane to stay over the correct side, divide it into bunches and secure the ends with a rubber band.

After the mane has been pulled, it will be ready for plaiting. This will not only make it neat, it will also show off the neck and crest, and keep the hair over on the off side. You will need a water brush, a bucket with a little water, some pieces of thread about 20 cm (8 in) long and the same colour as the mane, a needle with a large eye and a pair of scissors.

Damp down the mane with the brush and divide it into six equal parts. If the horse has a very long neck, more plaits may be needed. But there should always be an even number along the crest. Then plait each bunch of hairs. And when the plait reaches about three-quarters of the way down, a piece of thread should be plaited in with the remaining hairs. When the plait is completed, the ends of the thread should be looped round it and

pulled tight. Make sure that all the plaits are about the same length; if they are not, they can be shortened by making a further loop over.

Then put both ends of the thread through the eye of the needle. Doubling the end of each plait under, push the needle through it from underneath. Do this as close to the crest as possible. When the ends of the thread have been pulled through, the needle can be removed and the thread bound tightly round the plait and knotted at the top. The ends of the thread can then be cut off. Finish off by

A horse being shown to good advantage while jumping, not only because he has put in a good jump but also because the plaits show off the shape of his neck so well. Plaits enhance a horse's general smart appearance and look of efficiency.

combing and plaiting the forelock, which should come outside the brow band.

Plaiting a tail is an art, and is seldom done correctly. But it can enhance the look of a horse, particularly in the show ring, and is ideal if a tail is difficult to pull.

Boxing

If you are planning to go to a show, make sure that your horse will box easily. There is no point in getting him ready and then finding that he refuses to go into the box. You will have wasted your time and the entry fee.

If your horse has not been boxed, practise a few days before he is due to travel. Make sure that the ramp is not too steep. It should be on level ground, so that it will not sway and give way when the horse puts his foot on it.

You will certainly never drag a horse into a trailer or horse box. The proper procedure is to look straight ahead when you lead him to the ramp; many people, expecting trouble, fuss and shout to such an extent that the horse is hardly likely to have any confidence in what he is being asked to do.

A difficult horse may have had unhappy experiences in the past. His box may have been driven badly. And he has sufficient sense to realize that he is not only being asked to go up a ramp and stand in a confined space but also to face the bumps and bangs and the noise and swaying that will follow. He will need to be persuaded that travelling in a box need not be as unpleasant as he fears.

If you have the time, place the box or trailer near his stable with the ramp down and some straw on it. At feed time, when he is hungry, take him over to the box and put his feed bowl on the end of the ramp so that he has to put his feet on the ramp to eat. For subsequent feeds, move the bowl progressively further up the ramp until eventually he will follow you up into the box.

If there is a horse available that is always easy to box, he can help with a difficult horse. Get someone to lead him up into the box so that your horse sees him entering. Make sure the partitions are in such a position that your horse can walk straight into his stall. Make a fuss of him, and let him have a titbit so that he knows that by going into the box he gets a reward.

When the ramp is up, stay and make a fuss of him. Make sure that the driver takes the box carefully into corners and round traffic islands, so that the horse is not pitched forward or thrown off balance. He must have enough room in the box to be able to put his feet out to balance himself properly and wedge his quarters against the side. Many horses become frightened of travelling because they have been carried in boxes with partitions that were too narrow for them to get a proper foothold.

Overcoming problems with boxing

There are a number of dodges for getting horses into boxes. I have seen some of them tried with varying degrees of success. But gaining a horse's confidence, and letting him know that he has nothing to fear by going into a box is really the only solution.

One trick that is sometimes used in racing stables can be effective. But it should only be tried in a desperate situation when a horse refuses to box to go home, and no other way will work.

Take a piece of cord and make a loop at one end of it. Pass the cord over the horse's head and let the loop hang about level with his cheekbone. Then bring the cord up under the horse's upper lip and pass it through the loop.

Ask someone to stand behind the horse as you lead it to the ramp, hold the end of the cord in your hand, and if he attempts to resist your efforts to lead him into the box tighten the cord slightly and get your assistant to give the horse a good slap on his quarters.

The horse will usually be too concerned about the cord to worry about any dangers he may feel could be lurking in the box. When he moves forward, loosen the cord slightly. If he tries to resist, tighten it gently.

This method was first used, as far as I know, at the old Cavalry School at Netheravon. The cord can be used over a bridle or headcollar. But care must be taken that it is not too thin, and it must be emphasized that this method should only be used when all else has failed. Get advice from someone who knows about the method before you try to use it yourself.

Never let anyone stand to one side of the ramp when you are leading a horse into the box. The horse's normal reaction is to move away from anyone he feels might do something to hurt or frighten him, and he could slip off the side of the ramp and get hurt.

If you have enough helpers, station them behind the horse's quarters and on either side and let them move forward together as you walk the horse towards the ramp. In that way, the horse will be encouraged to go straight.

Never travel a horse in a box unless he has proper protective clothing. Make sure you take everything needed for his wel-fare, including food and water. Do not rely on other people's water troughs. In addition, all the necessary saddlery, bandages, boots and studs must be remembered. Always carry a medicine chest in case of cuts and knocks, and take an extra headcollar and rope.

Care at a show

Leave plenty of time to get to the event well before the hour that your horse is due to perform. This will enable him to have a less hurried and less tiring journey, and will allow for unforeseen hold-ups on the way. It will also give him time to settle down in his new surroundings so that he will be ready to do himself and you justice when it is his turn to go before the judges. After a journey by box, he will probably want to stale. He will be more likely to do so if he is tied up to the side of the box on the grass, or is led around.

Never let a horse graze at a show. If he has done well, give him a piece of apple or a handful of grass from the verge, but do not let him eat the grass from a field

Before leading a horse from a horsebox, it is important to make sure that the ramp is on level ground, and that the side gates are securely fixed. A ramp that is unsteady can make a horse nervous.

where other animals may have grazed. If they happened to have been suffering from a virus disease, your horse could be put out of action for weeks.

For the same reason, it is unwise to let him touch noses and get into too close proximity with other competitors' horses. They may look fit enough, but they may be sickening for something, or have come from a stable which already has coughing.

It is better to be safe than sorry, even though you may appear to be rather unsociable. There will be plenty of time to talk to other people when your horse is safely back in his box and munching his own hay.

Riding across country
If a horse is to be ridden over fences across country, bandage his legs well using gamgee underneath the bandages, and put some petroleum jelly on the front of his legs and stifle. When he has completed the course, he will no doubt be blowing, even if he is fit. Jump off as soon as he has finished, loosen the girth, and walk him back to the box. He will probably be excited and fidgety, so let him cool off both mentally and physically. Take off his saddle and bridle and put on his headcollar; then sponge him down using cold water and a sweat scraper. Wash his mouth and lips with a clean sponge and cool water. Put a sweat rug over him, and walk him round until he is cool and has stopped blowing. Because he will be inclined to fidget when you are walking him round, the sweat rug will have to be kept in place with a roller.

When you are sure he has dried off and is warm (feel his ears and make sure they are not cold), he can have his rug on and his studs removed. His leg and tail bandages can then be put on ready for the journey home and he can have a titbit if he has done well. But never give a horse anything to eat, not even a peppermint or a piece of apple, until he has stopped blowing. Provided that he has nothing more to do, your horse can have a short drink of water and a small feed, well dampened down. Do not give him his hay net until at least an hour after the finish of the cross-country. It is better to keep it for him to eat on the way home.

Care after the show
After a horse has been galloping and jumping, his tendons and other leg muscles will be tired, and it is advisable to treat his legs with Animalintex or a solution of some such substance as Armoricaine before putting the bandages on to go home. If not, treat his legs as soon as you return to the stable.

Take a small primus stove with you to heat a kettle of water if you are going to use Animalintex. You will also need an old bucket and some rubber gloves to mix the Armoricaine with water until it becomes a paste. Then spread it thickly on the back of the legs from behind the knee to the fetlock and leave it to dry. It will brush off quite easily the following day.

If you are doing a lot of cross-country work, the Armoricaine—which helps tighten up the muscles and prevent puffiness in the legs—may cause a slight irritation. To avoid this, use Animalintex on some occasions and Armoricaine on others.

When the horse arrives back in the stable, run him up to see that he is sound. If the weather is mild and it is not too dark, keep the bandages on, but take his rugs off and let him into the paddock for a quick roll and a nibble of grass. He will appreciate the opportunity of stretching his muscles and relaxing for a few minutes.

He will then be ready for his evening meal and haynet. Leave the Animalintex or Armoricaine on overnight, but make sure the bandages are not too tight and cannot be pulled off.

The next day, he can be given gentle walking exercise to loosen him up. Taking trouble with his legs after a competition will help to keep your horse sound.

13: Vices and their treatment

Many bad habits and vices may not show up in a horse until some time after it has been purchased, and their causes may be difficult to trace. But most stable vices result from boredom. A horse looks around for a way of occupying his time and does something that he finds amusing. Unless action is taken, a habit can develop quickly.

Sometimes, vices, such as rug stripping or kicking a stable door, are not particularly bad. One such vice is windsucking, in which the horse usually stands with his head raised and his neck strangely arched, sucking in and swallowing air with a peculiar characteristic noise. Sometimes, while he is sucking hard, he will curl his tongue over his lips.

Crib biting

Crib biting is a vice often associated with windsucking. The horse grabs hold of a manger (or any other projection, such as the bar of a gate) with his teeth. At the same time, he makes a strange sucking noise. The fronts of the incisor teeth get worn down and look rather like the bevelling on a chisel. Most crib biters give themselves away, particularly when they are put into a fresh stable. Sometimes, it is possible to tell whether a horse has this vice by looking at his teeth to see whether the incisors have become rounded.

Because crib biting and windsucking often cause digestive problems and chronic crib biters lose condition and are difficult to keep fit, they are particularly serious vices. Various devices have been designed to counter crib biting.

The most frequently used is a crib strap. This consists of a thick leather shield that fits into the gullet and is held in position by an adjustable strap, passing round the nose.

The flute bit is a hollow, perforated mouthpiece that disperses the air as the horse gulps, and prevents it being sucked in. There is also a cribbing device made from vulcanite; it has a soft rubber centre, and is fastened tightly round the gullet by a strap which passes over the poll and is attached to the headcollar.

There is no known cure for crib biting. The simple answer, if you want to keep the horse, is to put him in a stall or loose box where there is nothing for him to grab with his teeth. Mangers that hang over doors are, I am sure, a potential cause of crib biting, unless they are taken away the moment a horse has finished his food. He will otherwise lick round it and start to chew the lip. Eventually, if you are unlucky, he will begin to hold the manger with his teeth, and the trouble will start. If you look at the lips of some plastic mangers that have been in use for some time you will see the teeth marks.

Weaving

Weaving is an even more strange and wearing habit. A horse will stand at a stable door, moving his head from side to side like a pendulum and at the same time shifting his weight from one foot to another. Some people do not regard weaving as a serious vice. But, like a windsucker or a crib biter, an animal that weaves will probably soon pass on the habit to other horses in a stable. A weaver would have to be a very brilliant horse indeed for me to want to keep one with other horses present.

A means that may stop an animal from weaving is to suspend two thick cords over the door of the loose box with a brick tied to each end. There should be just enough room for the horse to put his head between the cords. As he moves his head from side to side, the bricks will start to sway and will bang against his neck and shoulders. The irritation, coupled with the knocks from the bricks, can sometimes make a horse think better of the habit.

Some owners, however, either put a grill over the door or have two metal bars placed vertically so that the horse cannot move his head from side to side when he puts it between the bars to see outside. Really bad weavers will weave inside the stable even when the top of the door has been closed.

There are very few perfectly mannered horses or ponies, but owners would be wise to try to ensure that any horse they buy is free of these very annoying and sometimes harmful habits, which, once they have become really established, are almost impossible to cure.

A stable showing obvious signs of a horse that has been crib biting, probably because of boredom. When considering a horse for purchase, a lot can be learnt from the appearance of his stable and his general behaviour and stable manners. Old stables, however, can bear the marks of many horses, and their present occupants are not necessarily the ones to blame.

14: Ailments and remedies

Horses are less likely to become ill if they are fed and handled properly, and if there is sensible stable management. Unfortunately, however, even horses that are well looked after sometimes get injured or become ill.

When that happens, the sensible answer is usually to get professional advice. But, of course, it is helpful to be able to recognize ailments before they become firmly established. And there are illnesses that are not too serious which will usually respond quickly if an owner knows what action to take.

The most frequent causes of ailments and injuries are bad conformation, bad feeding, bad facilities, bad stable management and boredom. Bad conformation is difficult to deal with because it is inherent in a horse. It might have been wiser not to have bought the animal in the first

place. Although a skilled farrier can help to alter a horse's action by special shoeing, serious weaknesses are bound to show up in time when tackling strong work such as hunting, racing or cross-country riding. Bad feeding can be avoided; but it is still the cause of many of the most prevalent forms of illness in horses and ponies.

Colic
This term is used to describe any type of abdominal pain. It may range from a mild attack of indigestion to a serious stoppage in the bowels, or even a twisted gut.

The first indication of colic is usually that the horse shows obvious signs of discomfort, lying down frequently and getting up again, swishing his tail and periodically looking towards his flanks. He may roll or lie flat out and then get up and try to stale or pass dung.

Unfortunately the symptoms of mild indigestion and those of the serious forms of colic are very similar in the early stages. In severe disturbances or a stoppage in the bowels, however, they will soon become acute—even to the extent of the animal becoming violent and throwing himself about. He may also go down on his hind legs and try to crouch rather like a dog. The membrane of his eye will turn from pink to a dark colour.

In severe cases, as the pain increases, the pulse rate—which can be checked by putting a finger on the submaxillary artery at the point where it passes under

If a horse shows any symptoms of colic a vet must be called immediately, and the horse kept warm and walked gently round the stable yard to prevent him lying down.

the jawbone—may rise to more than 80 or 90 beats a minute. The normal rate is 36 to 40 beats a minute.

A veterinary surgeon must be called immediately. Symptoms of colic should never be treated lightly, because colic is an illness that can prove fatal. Colic drenches may relieve symptoms but do not always cure the trouble. It is far better to keep the horse warm with additional blankets, and to walk him slowly round until the arrival of a veterinary surgeon. At the same time try to prevent him from lying down or kicking out at his stomach.

Indigestion is more prevalent in horses than many owners realize. It can be caused by worms, but often it is due to a badly balanced diet, musty food, irregular feeding, insufficient exercise, bolting down large quantities of dry food when the animal is tired and hungry, or perhaps drinking a lot of very cold water when he is overheated and sweating.

A stoppage of the bowels is generally due to the horse eating something that the stomach cannot deal with properly, such as decaying weeds, or hay that is heated or musty. The condition can be dangerous, because the veterinary surgeon may not always be able to reach the obstruction to remove it.

Fortunately, a twisted gut is relatively rare, but it is usually fatal. It may be caused by a heavy fall when the intestines are full of food, or by a horse throwing himself down in a severe attack of colic, or by the administration of too strong a purge when there is a stoppage in the bowels. The twist can occasionally be cured by surgery, but this is fraught with difficulty. Revolutionary progress has been made in bone surgery, but internal surgery still presents a problem.

Worms

Red Worms or *Strongyles*. There are several varieties, and a horse's intestines are a natural breeding ground for them. Some live in the intestines, and not only take the nourishment from the food but also cause anaemia when they stick to the walls of the intestine and suck the blood. The larval stages, particularly in young horses, enter the blood stream and can cause damage to intestinal blood vessels—giving rise to a thrombosis.

Horses with worms often have irregular bowel action, and any diarrhoea gives off a very offensive smell. There is also loss of condition, a distension of the stomach, anaemia and a dry and harsh appearance to the coat.

A sample of the animal's droppings must be analysed to see which type of medicine is necessary. The analysis should be done by a veterinary surgeon, who can prescribe the most effective treatment.

Red worms must be kept in check or they will cause serious trouble. Prevention is better than cure, and all horses at grass must be wormed at least three times a year, particularly in the spring, summer and autumn. Droppings should be picked up frequently from the field to stop the worms' eggs from hatching and infesting the land. Grazing cattle regularly is another method of keeping the ground sweet. Stabled horses need to be wormed even more frequently.

The *Seat Worm* or *Oxyuris* may not be injurious to health, but the worms lay eggs close to the anus, and cause irritation; consequently, they are a nuisance. One symptom is the horse trying to rub his tail.

Bots. Although not strictly worms, bots are parasites that live inside the stomach; they may have to be removed with one of the anti-worm preparations. The bot itself is a pupa which matures about springtime and detaches itself from the lining of the stomach before passing out with the animal's droppings. Soon afterwards, it develops into a large fly rather like a hornet but without a sting. The female lays eggs on the horse's coat, usually in the leg region; these can be seen quite clearly on horses at grass. A horse licks the coat, transferring the eggs into the stomach, and the cycle begins again. There are various methods of dealing with bot fly eggs, but probably the most effective is to use a safety razor; the eggs can then be carefully shaved off the coat with only a little of the hair being removed.

Skin diseases

Lice can be a problem with horses in poor condition particularly when they get into the mane or the base of the tail. They are brown, about 2 mm in length, and cause a great deal of itching. They result in bald, sore patches where the animal has rubbed himself to try to soothe the irritation. The lice can be removed by using one of a wide range of animal insecticides.

Ringworm is another irritating condition of the skin, causing circular, bald patches, which often become red and inflamed. It is particularly unpleasant because it is contagious to human beings as well as to animals. The disease is not caused by a worm but by a fungus. If you think an animal has ringworm consult your veterinary surgeon immediately. Keep the horse away from other horses. Isolate his tack, rugs and grooming kit, and wash your hands in disinfectant after any contact with him, his stable, or tack.

Sweet itch is not as serious, but is bad for a horse's well-being and appearance because it causes intense irritation. There is also baldness, thickening and inflammation of the skin around mane and tail. Small midges cause sweet itch, which occurs only during the summer months. Some animals are much more susceptible than others, and it can be hereditary. Most likely, the disease occurs when a horse or pony is particularly sensitive to the bites of certain insects. An affected animal should be kept indoors during the periods of the day when the insects are more likely to be about. Treating the sore patches is difficult; but if a horse is susceptible to sweet itch and is being turned out, there are medicinal solutions that are effective when rubbed into the mane and tail at frequent intervals. They make the tail look greasy; but that is better than bare patches.

Mange, fortunately, is now a rare condition. It is caused by a type of parasite that affects the skin in the area of the mane, legs and tail. There may be a slight swelling in the legs and an irritating rash; these will be evident because the horse will stamp and try to bite the affected part. Grooming kits, bandages and other items of equipment that have been in contact with the affected horse should be disinfected. The veterinary surgeon should be consulted before diagnosis is made.

Humour or *hives*. This is another skin condition that may be encountered. It is seen as numerous weals, or plaque-like swellings under the skin. It is caused by internal digestive disturbances, or by external influences such as nettlerash. Antihistamines may be required, but most

A horse suffering from a particularly bad case of sweet itch, a very uncomfortable and unsightly ailment. When sweet itch is as advanced as this, it is rather too late for the application of one of the various medical solutions that prevent the horse rubbing. But the animal could be taken indoors away from the sun and flies.

cases will respond to the administration of bran mashes and Epsom salts.

Girth galls are a fairly common problem, particularly with fat ponies, whose skin is soft because they are unfit. They are areas of skin, usually around the girth, that become thickened and sore. Cushioning the girth is sometimes the answer, but the pony should not be ridden until the sore patch improves. I have found a piece of clean motorcycle inner tube placed over the girth in the affected area can help to relieve the soreness and friction. It also allows the hair to grow even when the pony is ridden.

Warts. Young horses sometimes suffer from warts, mainly on the muzzle. They are unsightly and a nuisance; but they can disappear as quickly as they arrived, and they rarely affect a horse beyond the age of six.

Mud fever. Horses with white hair on their legs tend to be more liable to this annoying inflammation of the skin. All horses, however, can suffer from the affliction, which occurs mainly on the lower part of the limbs. There is usually puffiness and heat in the legs, and the skin gets sore, rough and scabby. In severe cases, the animal can go lame. The legs must be kept dry and free from mud. If they need to be washed, they should be dried with a chamois leather or warm cloth. The veterinary surgeon will probably prescribe a soothing lotion or cream, such as zinc ointment or lanolin.

Cracked heels can be treated in much the same way. Cracks appear in the hollow at the back of the pastern, and the skin becomes red, sore and scabby. If a horse is very susceptible to cracked heels, white petroleum jelly or lanolin should be applied to the heels before the horse goes out for exercise.

Bacterial and viral infections
Strangles used to be an extremely serious disease, particularly among ponies in poor condition. It is very contagious, and can be passed from one horse or pony to another–not only by direct contact, but also through anything the affected animal has touched, including a stable building or field shelter. A horse with strangles will go off his food and have a fever. Swellings will appear on either side of the throat, and there can be difficulty in breathing. An obvious sign may be a nasty, thick, white discharge from the nose.

The horse must be isolated, and everything he comes into contact with must be disinfected and washed, including your own clothing. He will need to be kept warm, and a veterinary surgeon must be called as quickly as possible. After the

The lymph nodes on a horse's throat being examined as a precautionary measure. If they show signs of being swollen, the cause may be a respiratory infection of some kind, and not necessarily a serious and infectious illness such as strangles.

horse has recovered, his bedding must be burnt, and the stable walls scrubbed with strong disinfectant.

Coughs, Colds and Influenza. Horses are very susceptible to these ailments. The treatment can vary according to the cause, but the wisest course at the first sign of any cough, particularly if it is accompanied by a temperature and any unusual nasal discharge–some horses always have a slightly runny nose–is to consult a veterinary surgeon. On no account must the horse be worked. Influenza is a contagious virus infection, and there are various inoculations that can be quite effective.

Broken wind is a term covering various chronic lung conditions. If it is caused by an allergy, its effects can be alleviated by avoiding anything that causes dust in the stable, like poor quality straw, and by avoiding too many bulk foods, which must in any case always be fed dampened. Linseed oil about three times a week can also help, and the animal should be bedded down on good quality shavings, free from dust. In some cases, horses will have to be fed hay substitute cubes. The symptoms of a broken wind are a deep, persistent cough, and the horse's flanks can be seen to heave twice during exhalation.

Whistling, which can be hereditary, only occurs in larger horses. It is a condition that follows paralysis of one of the nerves of the larynx: the horse makes a high-pitched whistle when breathing in, particularly during fast work. If this causes respiratory distress, it may be helped by the Hobday operation. The membrane from the pouch behind the vocal cord is removed so that the cord sticks to the wall of the larynx and the horse can breathe freely.

Ailments of the legs and feet

Capped knees and capped hocks can result from a blow to the knees or hocks. They may be treated by rest, hosing or poulticing, and a mild blister if the swelling persists.

Azoturia is sometimes known as 'Monday sickness' because it was particularly prevalent among van horses who were left on full rations without exercise on Sundays, and then taken out for hard work on Monday. Cramp in the muscles of the loins and quarters may make the horse stop or move only with great difficulty. He will sweat and have a temperature, and his breathing will be faster than usual. If he is able to stale, the urine may be brown in colour.

If the attack occurs away from the stables, transport will be needed home. He must be kept warm, and given plenty of water and a laxative diet, such as a warm bran mash. If possible, gentle heat should be played onto the affected areas, and the veterinary surgeon will probably give him an injection to relax the muscles. Because Azoturia can recur, particular care must be taken over the exercise and diet of any horse that has been affected.

Whenever a horse is unfit for work, he

Cold hosing is a useful method of removing heat from the legs. Such heat can have a variety of causes. It may be in the knees or fetlock joints, or, in the case of a horse that has jarred his legs, it could be in the tendons. Cold water should be allowed to trickle gently from a hose over the affected area.

must be treated with a laxative diet to prevent such problems as Azoturia when work restarts. Many leg and foot problems could also be prevented by better stable management or a little more care when a horse is turned out.

Thrush is a disease of the frog of the foot; there is a nasty-smelling discharge. Thrush usually occurs because the feet have not been picked out properly, and bedding has been allowed to get dirty and damp.

The frog and cleft of the foot will need cleaning with soap and water. When the frog area is dry, Stockholm tar should be applied to the affected area.

Corns, a frequent cause of lameness in horses, are really bruises that appear in the foot, near the heel, between the frog and the wall. They can usually be cured by removing the shoe and cutting away the horn over the affected area until the discoloration of the bruise appears. Then the shoe can be replaced. Some horses seem to suffer from corns far more than others. This is particularly true of hunters shod with short-heeled shoes. The condition is recognizable by a blood-red coloration of the horn.

Canker is a more serious condition. Various parts of the hoof become spongy and give off a grey or white discharge. The advice of a veterinary surgeon should be sought as soon as possible.

Sandcracks may appear when there is a split in the wall of a hoof that has become brittle. A skilled blacksmith can prevent the crack from opening further, and the horn can be encouraged to grow by the application of a mild blister to the coronet band. Or Cornucrescine can be applied to the hoof with a soft, clean brush.

Laminitis is a much more serious disorder of the feet. It is also called 'fever of the feet', because there is inflammation of the sensitive tissues lining the inside wall of the foot. It is caused by too much rich food, particularly lush grass, or lack of adequate exercise.

Horses with flat feet and weak horns are particularly susceptible. Any animal with the disease will indicate that he is in acute pain by a reluctance to move, and by standing with his weight on his heels. In chronic cases, ridges will form on the hoof because the horn will be produced irregularly. The shoes must be removed and the horse's feet cut down and hosed with cold water. The veterinary surgeon will also probably give an injection of painkillers. Great care will also have to be paid to diet.

Navicular disease is a disease of the navicular bones in the front feet caused by thrombosis in the local blood vessels. It may be the result of too much con-

Sand cracks should never be treated lightly because they can develop into a very serious condition if they are not dealt with quickly and efficiently. The treatment should be carried out in accordance with the advice of a veterinary surgeon or blacksmith. There are several effective methods of treatment, including nailing, wiring and the use of special shoes.

cussion on hard ground, and may have an hereditary origin. An X-ray will be needed to confirm the diagnosis. Treatment consists of the use of such painkillers as Phenylbutazone; or even more drastically, the foot may have to be de-nerved by an operation that cuts through the sensory nerves. The symptoms of Navicular disease are, initially, intermittent lameness and a habit of pointing the affected foot in the stable. The hoof may shrink to be slightly smaller than the others as the disease progresses.

The disease has always been considered to be incurable, but now new treatments are being tried with very encouraging signs of success. Fortunately, some horses who once suffered from Navicular disease are now working normally again.

Pedal Ostitis is a serious complaint caused by bruising of the pedal bone, mostly in the forelegs, when a horse has been ridden hard on firm or stony ground. A six months' rest on soft ground together with special diets will usually produce a cure.

Splints are bony enlargements of the splint bone on each side of the cannon. They are the result of blows, or occur when a young horse has been given an excessive amount of hard work. Unless the splint is pressing on the knee joint or the suspensory ligament, cold treatment and rest will usually cure any lameness. If the lameness persists, the splint may need to be pin fired or blistered.

Bone spavin is an enlargement of the bone on the lower and inner side of the hock. In the early stages of the condition, any lameness usually wears off with exercise: but the hock will move stiffly, and the horse will drop his hind toe. Excessive work in the case of young horses, particularly those with cow, sickle or weak hocks, is the most frequent cause. The condition is permanent. A long rest may be necessary, and either blistering or pin firing.

Bog spavin is a fluid distension of the joint capsule which shows up as a soft swelling on the inner side of the hock at the front. Heat is not usually present, and lameness will only occur if the swelling interferes with the horse's action. Shoeing with high heels and rolled trees will help to relieve the strain; and rest, cold treatment and pressure bandaging may be necessary if the horse becomes lame.

Curb, which rarely causes lameness, is a swelling seen below the point of the hock as a result of a ligament becoming enlarged. This again can be caused by young horses being given too much galloping and jumping. Rest is the best cure, but inflammation can be relieved by poulticing and cold-water treatment.

Thoroughpin is a small swelling above and in front of the point of the hock. Larger thoroughpins can go through from one side of the hock to the other. If the thoroughpins become too large, they should be rested and blistered.

Ringbones. Bony enlargements of the pastern bones caused by sharp blows or other local damage are called ringbones. There is a tendency for heat and pain to develop when the animal is worked on hard ground. A high ringbone above the coronet can be felt, but a low ringbone in the region of the coronet may need an X-ray diagnosis. If lameness persists, cortisone can be injected; and blistering may be necessary, as well as corrective shoeing.

Sidebone, which is an ossification of the lateral cartilage of the foot, can usually be felt, and is caused by concussion. Lameness does not usually occur unless there is pressure on a sensitive area. Blistering may be necessary if rest and cold treatment does not succeed.

Sprained tendons. Heat and swelling are always present with sprained tendons, and in bad cases the back of the leg can look bowed. Accurate diagnosis is important because swellings in the leg may be caused by other problems elsewhere. Rest is essential. Blistering or firing was at one time looked upon as an essential part of the treatment, but whenever possible other remedies are now usually preferred.

Sprained fetlock joints. Horses with upright joints that are not very elastic in their movements are susceptible to sprained fetlock joints. The heat and swelling around the joints should be treated by rest and hot and cold poultices.

Wounds

Mouth injuries. Salt and water washes are good for all mouth injuries. If the horse is to be worked, a bitless bridle will be needed instead of a normal bit until the injury heals.

All wounds should be cleaned with salt water or an alternative mild antiseptic solution and dressed with a topical wound powder. Do not hose initially, as this may drive dirt or grit deeper into the wound. Strong antiseptics and disinfectants are not recommended because they can kill

the healing cells as well as any harmful germs. Any hair in the way should be clipped without allowing it to fall into the wound. The injury may require stitching, and it should be protected with lint and a layer of cotton wool held in place with a bandage.

In any open injury there is a danger of tetanus, which can be fatal. If the horse has not already been vaccinated, he should be given an anti-tetanus injection without delay.

Swellings can be reduced by hot and cold fomentations. A swelling developing in the area can be the first signs of an infection that would need immediate professional treatment.

Any severe haemorrhage must be dealt with quickly, and the veterinary surgeon called immediately. The blood from a torn artery will spurt out bright red, but from a vein the flow will be steadier and much darker. If a leg is injured, a pressure pad should be applied to the wound. If the blood is pumping out (arterial), a tourniquet may be applied above the knee. It must not be put on too tightly, and will have to be released for a few seconds every 15 minutes to allow blood to circulate.

Do not ever hesitate to send for a veterinary surgeon when your horse is ill or injured. An early visit can save money – and in some cases a horse's life.

It is always wise to feel the tendons of a horse after he has returned from exercise, and particularly after he has been galloping and jumping. Any heat or puffiness must be dealt with immediately. Tendons should be approximately parallel to the cannon bone and bound tendons will spring outwards. Strained tendons, which usually require cold water treatment and rest, are mostly found only in the forelegs.

Index